QUINTA
DE LA ROSA

DOURO

*Denominação
Origem Controlada*

2001

VINHO TINTO

RED WINE

PRODUCE OF PORTUGAL

ENGARRAFADO POR
QUINTA DA ROSA VINHOS DO PORTO LDA
5085 PINHÃO PORTUGAL

13,5% vol.   e 75cl

ALL ABOUT
WINE

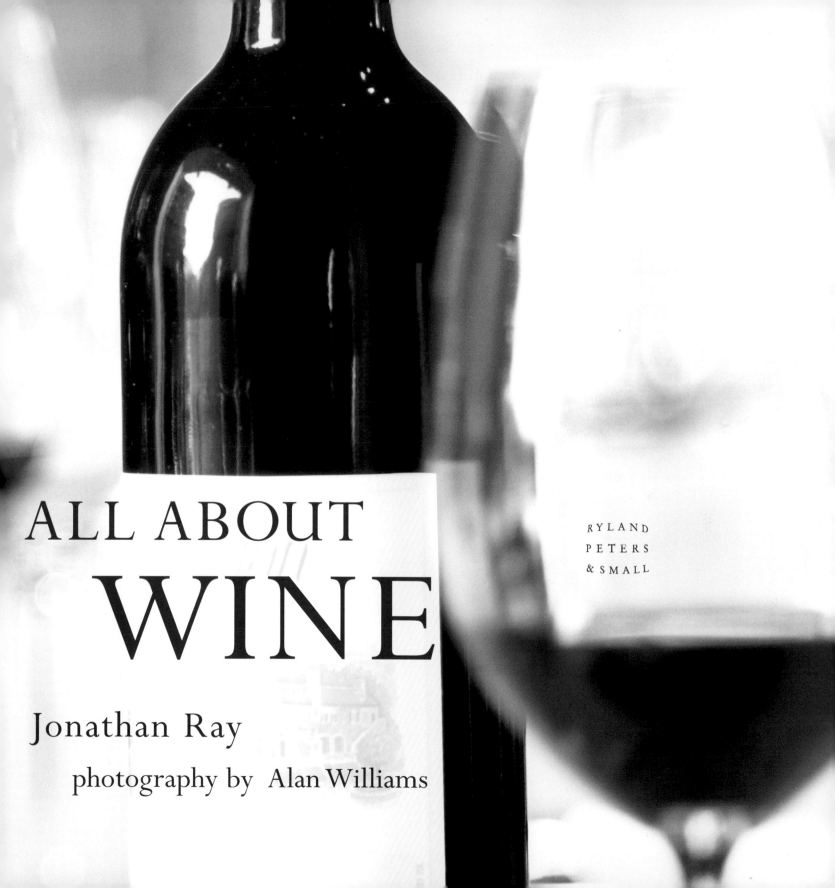

ALL ABOUT
WINE

Jonathan Ray

photography by Alan Williams

RYLAND
PETERS
& SMALL

Designer Pamela Daniels
Editor Miriam Hyslop
Production Gavin Bradshaw
Location Researcher Tracy Ogino
Art Director Gabriella Le Grazie
Publishing Director Alison Starling

U.S. Wine Consultant Tina Caputo
Illustrator Annie Boberg,
The Organisation www.organisart.co.uk

First published in the United States
in 2005 by Ryland Peters & Small, Inc.
519 Broadway, 5th Floor
New York, NY 10012
www.rylandpeters.com
10 9 8 7 6 5 4 3 2 1

Library of Congress Cataloging-in-Publication
Data

Ray, Jonathan.
  All about wine / Jonathan Ray.
    p. cm.
  Includes index.
  ISBN 1-84172-966-3
  1. Wine and wine making. I. Title.
  TP548.R2858 2005
  641.2'2--dc22

2005008647

Printed in China.

FOR FERDY AND LUDO, WITH LOVE.
I'M LOOKING FORWARD TO US
SHARING OUR FIRST BOTTLE
TOGETHER...

CONTENTS

INTRODUCTION 6

WINE BASICS 10

THE GRAPES 20

Red Grapes 22

Cabernet		Grenache	33
Sauvignon	25	Tempranillo	34
Merlot	26	Sangiovese	35
Pinot Noir	28	Pinotage	36
Syrah/Shiraz	30	Zinfandel	36
Cabernet Franc	32	Barbera	37
		Nebbiolo	37

Gamay	39
Malbec	39
Mouvèdre	40
Carignan	40
Cinsault	41
Petit Verdot	41

White Grapes 42

Chardonnay	44	Gewürztraminer	53
Sauvignon Blanc	46	Pinot Blanc	54
Sémillon	48	Pinot Gris	54
Riesling	51	Muscat	55
Chenin Blanc	52	Silvaner	55
		Aligoté	56

Viognier	56
Müller-Thurgau	57
Colombard	58
Roussanne	58
Marsanne	59
Trebbiano	59

KEY WINE AREAS 60

France	**62**	**Spain**	**88**	**Australia**	**120**
Bordeaux	64	Central Northeast	91	New South Wales	123
Burgundy		Central Northwest	92	Victoria	123
& Chablis	66	Central & Southern	94	South Australia	124
The Rhône	69	**Portugal**	**96**	Western Australia	125
Champagne	70	**Germany**	**100**	Tasmania	125
The Loire	72	**North America**	**104**	**New Zealand**	**126**
Alsace	75	California	107	**South Africa**	**130**
Rest of France	76	Pacific Northwest	110	**Other Areas**	**134**
Italy	**78**	New York State	110	**Dessert**	
North-west	81	Canada	111	**& Fortified**	**136**
North-east	82	**South America**	**112**		
Central	85	Chile	114		
Southern	86	Argentina	118		

MAKING THE MOST OF EVERY GLASS — 142

Choosing Wine by Style	144
Bottles & Labels	150
Where to Buy Wine	154
Putting Together a Cellar	156
Storing Wine	160
Glasses	162
Equipment	164
Opening, Decanting, & Serving	166
Ordering in a Restaurant	169
Tasting Wine	172
Wine Faults & Controversies	176
Wine & Food	178
Wine Words	184
Useful Websites	186

Business & Picture Credits	**186**
Index	**189**
Acknowledgments	**192**

This book is for those who have had a glass of wine and who would like another glass, but perhaps of something different. It is for those who want to learn a bit more about how and where the wine they have just drunk was made. And what could be more enjoyable than exploring the world of wine? After all, there can be few other subjects that consider uncorking (or unscrewing) a bottle and pouring yourself a glass to be an obligatory part of your research.

To the uninitiated, wine might seem a daunting subject best left to wealthy connoisseurs, but in truth it is accessible to everyone, and the basics can be learned in a matter of a few pleasurable hours. The appreciation of wine is, and always has been, a life-enhancing pleasure (even a life-prolonging one, for there is strong evidence that drinking wine is positively good for you) and it should be encouraged wherever possible. Plato was right when he said,

"Nothing more excellent or valuable than wine was ever granted by the gods to man."

The purpose of this book is to lead you gently by the hand on your journey of discovery, by introducing you to the major grape varieties and the regions in which they grow, and by explaining how wine is made, how it should be stored, how it should be served, and how it should be tasted. It will also help you decide which dishes go well with which wines, and it will guide you through the intricacies of choosing from restaurant wine lists.

But although this book can teach you the difference between the Napa Valley and Navarra, Bordeaux and Burgundy, Cabernet Sauvignon and Sauvignon Blanc, it is only by tasting the wines yourself that you will be able decide which you like and which you don't, so keep a corkscrew and glass close at hand at all times.

Too many people take wine too seriously, often ostracizing others in the process, making them feel small because they supposedly don't know enough about this wonderful subject. Nobody knows enough. Wine is a living world, forever changing, and what you know today, may not be true tomorrow. Even one's own tastes change and where last year you couldn't get enough California Chardonnay, this year you might be hankering after New Zealand Sauvignon Blanc.

It is easy to mock those who say, "I don't know much about wine, but I know what I like." But if you know what you like then you are halfway to being an expert, and what other people think isn't important. This book aims to take you the remaining part of the way. If you know that you like Chardonnay (or Liebfraumilch, come to that), then spend a few minutes in finding out what other wines taste the same or vaguely similar. It is akin to learning how to appreciate art or music. If you know you like the paintings of Monet, then it is quite probable that you will also like the paintings of Renoir; if you know that you enjoy the music of Haydn, there's a good chance that you'll like Mozart as well. But don't stop there: listening to Mozart should give you the confidence to progress to Beethoven, Brahms, and Mahler, in the same way that a mid-priced Chardonnay should lead you to the joys of Chablis Grand Cru; Liebfraumilch might show you the way to the great Rieslings of the Mosel.

But memorable bottles of wine don't necessarily have to come from fine vintages or cost the earth. Drunk in the right company or alongside the right food, even the simplest and roughest of wines becomes extraordinary.

With *All About Wine* as your guide, a whole new world should open before you, as you gain the knowledge and the confidence to make informed decisions and choices when you buy your wine. Before long you will find yourself discussing whether you think the New World makes better wine than the Old World, the merits and demerits of screwcaps and whether champagne is all that it is cracked up to be. It should encourage you to discover and learn more and to appreciate that a bottle of wine is so much more than just a pleasant beverage; it represents the people who make the wine, the food they eat, the countries they live in and their history.

But don't take everything as gospel. Plow your own furrow, and remember, the Tower of London will not fall down if you pass the port to the right nor will the world end if you drink red wine with fish.

WINE BASICS

A little bit of background information goes

a long way to explaining the mysterious

and magical liquid in your glass.

WINEMAKING

THE SIMPLE EXPLANATION
Wine is fermented grape juice. It is no more complicated than that. Well, it is a bit more complicated than that, but that is the story in essence. Grapes are grown on a vine, in a vineyard. They are warmed by the sun and they ripen. They are picked and then they are crushed. The sugar in the grape juice then interacts with yeast and turns into alcohol. *Voilà*, you have wine. If you are satisfied with this explanation then feel free to skip the next few paragraphs, if not, read on for the technical bit.

THE GRAPES
There are thousands of different grape varieties that can be used to make wine, all but a few coming from the vine species, *Vitis vinifera*. The best known are white grapes such as Chardonnay, Sauvignon Blanc, Chenin Blanc, and Riesling, and red grapes such as Cabernet Sauvignon, Merlot, Syrah, and Pinot Noir. However, differences between each wine are caused not only by the diverse varieties of grapes used, each of which have their own distinct flavor, but also by the soil, the way in which the wine is helped on its way by the winemaker, and by the climate in general and the more specific vagaries of the weather.

THE VINEYARD

As any winemaker will tell you, fine wine is made in the vineyard. You can certainly make bad quality wine from good quality grapes, but you cannot make good quality wine from bad quality grapes. What happens in the vineyard is crucial. To start with, you need well drained, not necessarily overly fertile soil, in order to make the vine's roots dig deep for sustenance. Different soils suit different grapes, with Chardonnay favoring limestone or chalk, for example, and Riesling thriving on slate-based soils.

The vineyard needs to have the right aspect, with plenty of exposure to the sun in cool climate areas such as Champagne or the Mosel and not too much in hot areas such as Sicily or South Australia. How the vines are trained, in bushes, say, or in rows is also important. There needs to be enough rain (or in some cases, irrigation). Too little and the grape skins become too tough and they fail to ripen, too much and the grape juice is diluted or mildew sets in.

The term given to this mysterious combination of soil, aspect, climate, microclimate, drainage, gradient, and whatever else results in great wine being produced from this bit of ground, and lesser wine from that bit of ground three feet away, is the French word, *terroir*.

THE WINERY

The timing of the harvest is crucial, with the winemaker playing an annual game of brinkmanship with the weather, especially in areas of marginal climate. Pick too early and the grapes won't be ripe enough and pick too late and they risk being hit by rain, hail, or frost in cool climate vineyards as fall arrives, or being baked to a frazzle in hot climate ones.

After the grapes are picked, either by hand or by machine, they are taken to the winery. Practices vary the world over, but in essence the grapes are sorted, possibly de-stemmed, crushed, and then pressed. After this, fermentation ensues—in concrete or stainless steel vats or oak barrels—encouraged either by the natural yeasts present on the grapes or by the introduction of cultured yeast. Red wines are fermented with their skins, seeds, and pulp in order to gain maximum flavor, color, and tannin, while whites are generally not. Rosé wines are made from red grapes which have had minimal contact with their skins, although in rare cases, such as in Champagne, they can be made simply by blending white wines with red.

BLENDS AND SINGLE VARIETALS

A blended wine is one where the fermented juice of one variety is joined with that of another—or others—as in Bordeaux, where any given red wine might be a blend of up to five different varieties, or in the Southern Rhône, where Châteauneuf-du-Pape can be made from up to 13 different varieties.

The art of blending is to marry varieties together to make a wine greater than the sum of its parts. The process can also encompass different vintages blended to ensure that the wines always taste the same. This occurs in non-vintage wines, most non-vintage champagne, and port.

Strictly speaking, a single varietal is a wine made from one grape variety only. However, rules differ from region to region, and in truth, a single varietal might contain a small amount of another variety. For example, in Australia, 80 percent of the wine must come from the named variety, while in the U.S. it is 75 percent. In Europe, the phrase single varietal is not much used, but those wines that would qualify for the term must be made from 100 percent of the named variety.

In Europe, the trend has been to name the wines after the region or property of origin rather than after the variety used (except, notably, in Alsace and in the developing Vin de Pays regional wines from Southern France). It is here that it pays to have a little knowledge: if, for example, you know that you like single varietal Pinot Noir from Oregon, then it is helpful to know that all red burgundies such as Pommard, Vosne Romanée, or Aloxe-Corton are also single varietal Pinot Noirs.

The blending of different varieties occurs less frequently with white wines than it does with red. In France, for example, the great wines of the Loire, such as Sancerre and Pouilly Fumé are 100 percent Sauvignon Blanc, while Chablis and white burgundies such as Meursault, Puligny-Montrachet, or Pouilly-Fuissé are 100 percent Chardonnays. Champagne is usually a blend of three varieties, although producers do make champagnes from just Chardonnay or just Pinot Noir.

Some producers prefer the purity and intensity of single varietals while others believe that careful blending leads to greater subtlety and delicacy. There are strong arguments for both, arguments that get trotted out whenever two or more wine-makers are gathered together. Neither style is better than the other, they are just different, and just because you like the subtlety of this blend doesn't mean that you won't appreciate the purity of that single varietal.

AGING

Aging is the process by which wines settle down and develop after fermentation, mature and improve, and nowhere do they do this better than in oak barrels. Great differences between wines are achieved by the size of the barrel, the type of oak used (it might be French Limousin or Tronçais, American or, increasingly, Russian oak) and by whether it is old oak or new oak, or a combination of the two. New oak contains vanillin, which often leads wines that have been in barrels for any length of time to smell of vanilla.

Of white wines, Chardonnay is particularly well suited to spending time in oak, by which process it takes on a deeper color and fuller, softer, vanilla-like flavors. Most red grapes, such as Cabernet Sauvignon, Merlot, Syrah, Pinot Noir, Sangiovese, and Tempranillo benefit from periods in oak.

Some producers feel that oak is essential (some of the more unscrupulous even steep their wines in oak chips as a rather unsatisfactory short cut to achieving the unique flavor associated with oak) while others feel that the wood imparts too much flavor to their wines, and prefer to use inert stainless steel instead.

VINTAGES

The term vintage refers not only to the annual harvest and gathering in of the grapes, but also to the wine made from those grapes. And although some vintages are good and some are bad, the fact that a vintage date is recorded on a wine label should not be taken as a guarantee of the quality of that wine, but rather as simply a matter of record and a note of the wine's age. If in doubt as to the quality of a particular year, refer to a vintage chart.

If a blend of two or more vintages is used, the wine will be known as non-vintage or NV, and will show no date on the label, as is often the case with inexpensive wines and most champagnes. The skill, especially with champagne, is to blend wines from a number of different vintages in such a way as to ensure that the end product tastes the same each time, so that consumers can rely on a particular house style.

The New World is less susceptible to vintage variation, thanks to a generally reliable climate, although many new marginal vineyards are being planted where greater differences do exist. And although poor vintages are becoming rarer in Europe owing to improved technology, a late frost, hailstorms, or lack of sunshine can still mean the difference between success and failure for a vintage.

The very best wines can take between five and 25 years to mature, although nowadays there is a trend among winemakers to produce wine for relatively early drinking.

VINTAGE CHART

1 = VERY POOR   10 = OUTSTANDING   ● = KEEP   ◐ = DRINK & KEEP   ○ = READY

VINTAGE	78	80	81	82	83	85	86	87	88	89	90	91	92	93	94	95	96	97	98	99	00	01	02	03	04
RED BORDEAUX	7	4	6	10	7	8	8	5	8	9	10	5	4	6	7	9	9	6	8	7	10	7	8	9	
WHITE BORDEAUX	4	6	6	7	9	7	8	5	10	9	10	4	4	2	6	9	10	9	8	8	7	9	5	9	
RED BURGUNDY	9	7	6	5	7	9	7	7	8	9	10	8	6	9	7	9	9	7	8	9	7	8	9	9	
WHITE BURGUNDY	7	6	4	7	8	8	8	6	7	8	9	6	8	8	7	9	10	9	7	8	9	8	9	7	
CHABLIS	7	6	8	6	7	7	7	5	7	8	10	5	8	6	6	9	10	8	7	7	8	7	9	7	
RHONE	10	6	5	8	9	9	8	5	8	9	10	7	6	5	7	9	8	8	9	9	9	8	7	8	
CHAMPAGNE	5	4	7	9	7	9	6	4	8	9	10	6	7	6	5	8	9	8	9	8	9	7			
LOIRE	6	5	6	7	7	8	8	6	8	9	10	4	5	7	6	9	8	9	7	7	8	8	8	8	
ALSACE	5	4	7	5	9	8	7	5	8	10	10	5	7	8	6	9	8	9	8	7	9	7	9	8	
ITALY	9	5	5	8	7	9	8	7	9	7	10	6	6	7	7	8	8	10	7	9	8	8	5	8	
SPAIN	7	6	8	10	7	8	6	9	6	7	8	8	7	6	9	8	9	6	7	8	7	9	7	8	
PORTUGAL	7	9	5	10	9	8	6	5	8	7	7	7	5	4	7	8	6	6	7	6	9	9	8		
GERMANY	5	4	6	4	8	8	7	5	8	9	10	7	8	7	8	8	7	10	7	8	7	10	8	8	
NORTH AMERICA	8	8	6	7	7	9	7	8	8	7	8	9	8	7	8	7	10	7	9	9	8			8	
CHILE																	7	8	8	9	8	9	7	8	8
ARGENTINA																	7	9	6	9	8	8	7	8	8
AUSTRALIA	8	10	5	9	6	8	9	8	7	6	8	8	7	6	7	9	9	7	8	8	7	8	7	8	8
NEW ZEALAND		4	6	6	9	8	7	6	7	9	7	8	7	6	8	7	9	9	9	8	8	8	7	8	7
SOUTH AFRICA	7	7	6	7	5	7	7	7	8	7	6	8	9	8	7	9	7	8	8	7	7	8	8	8	8
VINTAGE PORT		7			6	8	8					7	8		9			8	7		9			8	

© Berry Bros. & Rudd, 2005. www.bbr.com

SPARKLING WINES

The most important way to make a wine fizz is called the Champagne Method or *méthode traditionelle* and is described in the pages on champagne (page 70), but there are other ways, too. With the Transfer Method, wines that have undergone their secondary fermentation in bottle are disgorged under pressure into tanks—the whole contents, not just the frozen plug—prior to filtering and rebottling. This method is widely used in the New World, and it produces very decent wines, albeit without the finesse and elegance of those made by the *méthode traditionelle*. This is a much less expensive process as it removes the time-consuming "riddling" (the turning and tilting of the bottle) and the costly freezing, disgorging, and topping up of each bottle individually.

The Tank Method, also known as the Cuve Close or the Charmat Process involves a secondary fermentation in a sealed tank rather than in a bottle. Most German Sekt is made this way which, while good, doesn't have such fine or long-lasting bubbles as wines that are made by the other methods. Carbonation is the cheapest and least effective method of injecting bubbles into wine via what the French jokingly refer to as a *pompe bicyclette*.

THE GRAPES

Although climate, soil, and methods

of production all make significant

contributions to the way a wine tastes,

the most important factor by far is

the grape itself.

RED GRAPES

There are four major red grapes—Cabernet Sauvignon, Merlot, Syrah, and Pinot Noir—all of which are seen all over the world.

Pinot Noir travels less well than the other three main varieties, and it has long been the winemakers' Holy Grail to produce wines that rival those from its homeland Burgundy. In their wake comes a supporting cast of less well-known, but important varieties that are more regionally based, such as Sangiovese which doesn't stray far from Italy, or Tempranillo, whose spiritual home is Spain.

There are other grapes that are even more closely linked with particular areas rather than countries, such as Gamay, almost the sole purpose of which is to produce the light, fruity, and jammy red wine of Beaujolais.

Some red varieties that have fallen, or are falling, out of favor in the Old World such as Malbec and Petit Verdot are finding a new lease of life in the New World, especially in South America. For the time being, this is one-way traffic, as the restrictive wine laws of Europe and resistance to change means that you are unlikely ever to see Pinotage (famous in South Africa) or Zinfandel (California's own red grape) grown in Burgundy or the Rhône.

In the Old World, red wines tend to be blended from several different varieties, red burgundy being a notable exception. In the New World, on the other hand, single varietals have dominated, although there has recently been a move towards more European-style blends, especially in Australia and Chile, as blending gives the winemaker more scope to create a well-balanced and complex wine.

And your $64,0000 question. Which major red grape produces a famous white wine? Pinot Noir, of course, which as well as its role in making the great red wines of Burgundy also plays a prominent part in making the world's most celebrated sparkling white wine—champagne.

CABERNET SAUVIGNON

Okay, this is the big one. Cabernet Sauvignon is, without doubt, the most cherished red grape variety in the world, acclaimed as the backbone behind the finest clarets of Bordeaux, and as the producer of the New World's finest single varietals.

This wine is instantly recognizable in the glass owing to its overwhelming aroma of black currants, its juicy, jammy flavors, and its structure, tannin levels, and complexity. It has the ability to age exceptionally well.

While Cabernet Sauvignon is the most important variety in Bordeaux, it is never used on its own there, claret producers believing that its qualities can only be enhanced by blending it with one or more of the Cabernet Franc, Merlot, Malbec, Petit Verdot quartet.

Cabernet Sauvignon is grown throughout Europe, notably in Italy where it is grown in Piedmont and Emilia-Romagna, and is used to great effect in Tuscany. It is also becoming popular in Spain where it is often blended with Tempranillo.

It was Cabernet Sauvignon that first brought California to the attention of the wine world, with the best examples usually coming from the Napa Valley and Sonoma County. Hitherto it has often been made as a single varietal (although many "100 percent Cabernet Sauvignons" include tiny amounts of Merlot and Cabernet Franc), but producers have recently been moving away from single varietals towards making so-called Meritage blends, similar in style to Bordeaux, and insisting on using French oak, too. Some producers even use Cabernet Sauvignon to make fortified, port-style wines.

In Australia, Cabernet Sauvignon becomes more black-currant-like than ever, particularly in Coonawarra in Southeast Australia, which is the most favored spot for growing the variety. Australia often blends Cabernet Sauvignon with Shiraz or Merlot. Chile produces some of the finest Cabernet Sauvignons, which are exquisitely dark and intense with extraordinary depth. Lighter wines of good—rather than fine—quality are also made now in New Zealand and South Africa.

STYLE

Deep purple in color, Cabernet Sauvignon is identifiable by its intense black currant bouquet and aromas of mint, eucalyptus, cherries, and tobacco. It has excellent tannin and powerful, complex flavors.

GOES WITH

Roast meats, broiled or barbecued steaks, game, and most cheeses.

FAMOUS CABERNET SAUVIGNONS

Red Bordeaux is the grape's finest hour with wines such as Ch. Lafite-Rothschild, Ch. Latour, Ch. Margaux, Ch. Palmer all being predominantly Cabernet Sauvignon. It is a crucial ingredient of Italy's "Super Tuscans" such as Sassicaia and Tignanello, California's Opus One, and Chile's Seña.

MERLOT

In the Médoc area of Bordeaux, Merlot is very much the junior partner to Cabernet Sauvignon's chairman of the board, being used in blends to soften the latter's dominance. On the right hand side of the River Garonne however, in St. Emilion, Pomerol, Fronsac, Bourg, and Blaye, it plays by far the greater role.

Merlot is noted for its voluptuous volume of fruit and richness, soft tannic structure, and its plum fruit characteristics.

While Merlot's great fame and reputation derive from the great wines of Pomerol and St. Emilion, it is increasingly being grown in the currently-fashionable Languedoc-Roussillon, and is an important grape in northeast Italy, especially in Friuli, Emilia-Romagna, Trentino-Alto Adige, and the Veneto, and is often a component of the "Super Tuscans," being blended with Sangiovese and Cabernet Sauvignon. At its lowest level, however, Italian Merlots can be unwelcomingly thin and light-bodied with alarmingly high acidity.

In the New World, unblended Merlot can make wines of great style. It is argued that America's best Merlot comes from Washington State, but there are some very popular versions in California, too—California Merlots being heavier and fuller than those of Bordeaux. In South America, Argentina makes some very good Merlots and those of Chile are much admired for their silky elegance—newer versions are worth aging, too.

Even though many people believed that New Zealand was only suited to making white wine, Merlot has recently become a great success. Plantings in Australia are limited, producers and consumers seeming to prefer Shiraz for single varietals or Cabernet Sauvignon for blends.

STYLE

Merlot is known for its aromas of cherry, plum, mint, and black currant. Its softness and suppleness make it ideal for blending with the firmer, more tannic Cabernet Sauvignon.

GOES WITH

Merlot from whatever country is ideal with any poultry dishes, simply cooked lamb, and soft cheeses.

FAMOUS MERLOTS

It is the main grape of St. Emilion, Pomerol, and Fronsac in Bordeaux, in such wines as Ch. Le Pin, Ch. Pétrus, Ch. Ausone, Ch. Pavie, Ch. Figeac, and Ch. Lafleur.

PINOT NOIR

Pinot Noir has been grown in Burgundy for centuries and—unblended—makes the region's world-famous red wines such as Clos Vougeot, Corton, Beaune, Gevrey-Chambertin, Nuits-St-Georges, Pommard, and Romanée-Conti. It also plays a major part in the wines of Champagne.

Notoriously, Burgundy is one of the most difficult wine regions of all to fathom, with wines of the same name being made by vast numbers of different growers, producers, and *négociants*. One thing, however, should make Burgundy the simplest of all regions to understand, and that is the fact that all its red wines (barring the very lowliest, such as Bourgogne Passe-Tout-Grains) are made from one grape and one grape only—Pinot Noir. And while it would be true to say that the gap between top-quality and low-quality burgundy is startlingly large, nowhere else in the world is the grape so successful. It may

put you off that old Pinot Noirs from Burgundy are often characterized by a notable smell of farmyards, but don't let it, because they taste sublime and are highly prized.

Pinot Noir does well in the Loire where it produces the charming red and rosé Sancerres, and in Alsace—a region better-known for its aromatic white wines—where the locals lap it up, so much so that it is rarely exported.

As winemakers never tire of explaining, Pinot Noir is a right so-and-so to grow, being a famously bad traveler and susceptible to mildew, rot, and frost. Unlike, say, Cabernet Sauvignon, which is a bit easy going, bedding down happily almost anywhere vines are grown. For centuries, the French told us that it couldn't be grown outside Burgundy, the Loire, or Champagne and we believed them until pioneering winegrowers in Oregon, of all places, proved them wrong.

Unlike Cabernet Sauvignon, which always tastes just about the same wherever it is grown, Pinot Noir can taste very different in its various habitats. The cool climate in regions such as Oregon or Carneros in California and Western Australia lends itself to producing vigorous wines with loads of raspberry fruit. New Zealand is fast gaining a reputation for producing some of the Southern Hemisphere's finest Pinot Noirs—especially in Marlborough where its wines are being packed with vibrant cherry-like flavors.

STYLE

New World Pinot Noir is rich and full-flavored, with an appealing bouquet of ripe cherries, plums, raspberries, and strawberries. In Burgundy, when mature, it takes on more complex aromas of chocolate, prunes, game, rotting vegetables, and violets.

GOES WITH

Oregon Pinot Noir goes well with salmon or tuna, while Old World examples are perfect with meat dishes and stews such as *boeuf bourgignon* (in which it is a crucial ingredient).

FAMOUS PINOT NOIRS

All red burgundies such as Aloxe-Corton, Beaune, Gevrey-Chambertin and Nuits-St-Georges. Also champagne. Best New World examples come from New Zealand and Oregon.

SYRAH/ SHIRAZ

Syrah dominates the Northern Rhône in the same way that Grenache dominates the Southern Rhône, and is responsible for producing such famous wines as the full-bodied Cornas, Côte Rôtie, and Hermitage, and the slightly lighter Crozes-Hermitage and St. Joseph.

Syrah (known in Australia and South Africa as Shiraz) almost certainly originated in the Middle East and was brought by the Romans to the Rhône Valley, where it continues to produce wines of stunning concentration and full-bodied intensity. Syrah is an easy grape to grow. It produces a reliable crop, is resistant to most pests and diseases, and does especially well in poor soils and warm climates, and so is able to flourish on the precipitous granite slopes dangling above the River Rhône. Not only does Syrah rule the roost in the Northern Rhône, it also plays a small but important part in Grenache territory in the Southern Rhône, by adding flavor, weight, and body to the wines of Châteauneuf-du-Pape. Syrah enjoys the heat and is thus also fast gaining a reputation for producing enjoyable and palatable wines in Southern France, especially in Languedoc-Roussillon.

The variety's other great stronghold is Australia, especially in the Barossa Valley, where it first arrived in the 1830s. Since then it has become the country's most widely planted grape. It is either made into lip-smacking blends alongside Cabernet Sauvignon or into long-lived single varietals, the most celebrated example of which is Penfolds Grange—a powerfully intense wine to rival the finest in the world.

Although it has yet to match its success in France and Australia, Syrah is now being planted with more regularity in California—either for Rhône-style blends or single varietals. The grape is also beginning to shine brightly in both South America and South Africa, particularly around Stellenbosch.

STYLE

Instantly identifiable by oodles of pepper and spice on the nose, combined with black-berries and plums. Syrah's burly, intense wines are packed with tannin and have the ability to age for decades.

GOES WITH

Syrah in all its forms goes well with cassoulet and barbecued food, braised dishes, or roasts. Its spiciness also complements strongly flavored dishes such as pepperoni pizza.

FAMOUS SYRAHS

Hermitage, Crozes-Hermitage, St. Joseph, Côte Rôtie, Cornas all in the Northern Rhône and, most famously in the New World, Australia's Penfolds Grange.

STYLE

Less tannic, less acidic, less full-bodied but more aromatic than its cousin Cabernet Sauvignon—its wines often smelling of black currant leaves.

GOES WITH

Chilled red Loires go well with salmon steaks or tuna.

FAMOUS CABERNET FRANCS

Bourgueil and Chinon in the Loire and, most famously of all, Ch. Cheval Blanc in Bordeaux.

CABERNET FRANC

In the Médoc in Bordeaux, Cabernet Franc is very much the understudy to Cabernet Sauvignon's top billing. It is grown not only to boost the flavor of its near namesake in the claret blends, but also, because it ripens earlier, as its substitute in the event that the lead performer is indisposed by the weather. Cabernet Franc takes a far more prominent role in nearby St. Emilion, where most wines are blended from Cabernet Franc and Merlot. One shouldn't forget that it comprises almost half the blend that goes to make one of the world's finest wines—Ch. Cheval Blanc.

Its performance is also taken more seriously in the Loire, where it enjoys the cool conditions, making early-maturing, light red wines such as Bourgueil, Chinon, Saumur-Champigny, and the delightful rosé Cabernet d'Anjou.

Even though Cabernet Sauvignon is firmly established in California, where the benign climate ensures that it rarely fails, the earlier ripening Cabernet Franc continues to be grown there only in small amounts as a flavor-boosting back-up. It is also used in the region's Bordeaux-style Meritage wines, and there is a scattering of producers who make single varietals from it, as there are in Australia.

Cabernet Franc can also be found in modest amounts in South Africa, Argentina, New York State, Washington State, New Zealand, and in Friuli, in northeast Italy.

GRENACHE

Grenache—the world's second most planted red variety—produces richly fruity wines, which are high in alcohol with pleasant hints of sweetness. Although ideal for blending with other varieties such as Cinsault, Carignan, Mourvèdre, and Syrah, it can produce wines of great complexity on its own. It is especially successful in producing rosés because of its low tannins and fruity flavor.

In France, Grenache is grown mainly in Languedoc-Roussillon and the Southern Rhône where it provides the core of most Châteauneuf-du-Pape blends as well as being the dominant variety in the wines of Gigondas and the region's sought-after rosés such as Tavel, Lirac, Côtes du Rhône, and Côtes du Ventoux.

In Roussillon, it helps make some of the great sweet wines—known as Vins Doux Naturels—such as Banyuls and Rivesaltes.

Grenache is Spain's most widespread red grape. Known there as Garnacha, it is an important part of the Rioja blend, where it softens Tempranillo's rougher edges. Unlike France, there are producers in Navarra who like to use Grenache on its own, to make soft, drinkable wines notably high in alcohol.

Plenty of Grenache is grown in Australia, especially in the Barossa Valley, where it is becoming popular as a single varietal. It is also gaining presence in California where it is used in Rhône-style blends.

STYLE

High alcohol, low tannin wines with a jammy, juicy spiciness.

GOES WITH

Châteauneuf-du-Pape should be drunk with hefty meat dishes, such as wild boar or venison, or with strong cheeses. New World Grenache is an excellent match with barbecue.

FAMOUS GRENACHES

Châteauneuf-du-Pape, Gigondas, Tavel rosé in the Rhône; and often as part of the Rioja blend.

TEMPRANILLO

Tempranillo is to Spain what Cabernet Sauvignon is to France; it puts the grit into the country's most highly regarded red wines, most famously as the major component of Rioja.

Tempranillo is found throughout Spain, and although it is sometimes made into single varietal wines, it is usually blended with other varieties. In its strongholds of Rioja Alta and Rioja Alavesa, for example, it is blended with Garnacha (Grenache), Mazuelo, Graciano, and Viura. In Ribera del Duero, combined with the varieties that produce claret in Bordeaux, it makes Spain's finest wine—Vega Sicilia. The major red variety in Valdepeñas and La Mancha (where it is known as Cencibel), it is also grown in Costers del Segre, Utiel-Requena, Navarra, Somontano, and Penedès.

Tempranillo is most closely associated with Spain, but it can also be found in the Midi in France, in Portugal—where, known as Roriz, it is one of the many varieties used in the production of port—and in South America, especially in the Mendoza region of Argentina.

STYLE

A spicy, juicy wine that is well suited to oak-aging, picking up aromas of vanilla as it does so.

GOES WITH

Rioja goes especially well with rich meat dishes such as braised dishes, roast duck, goose, and lamb.

FAMOUS TEMPRANILLOS

Red Rioja is made from Tempranillo as is Spain's finest wine—Vega Sicilia.

SANGIOVESE

Along with Nebbiolo, Sangiovese is regarded as one of the two top red grapes in Italy, and is the most widely planted red grape in the country.

Sangiovese's heartland is in the central and southern regions of Italy but, despite the grape's high reputation, it must be said that the quality of its wines can vary dramatically, largely because so many different clones of the variety exist.

However, whatever its perceived shortcomings elsewhere might be, Sangiovese does, unquestionably, make the finest red wines of Tuscany. It is here that Chianti is made, with Sangiovese providing up to 90 percent of the blend. Chianti Classico is the highest quality Chianti, and often tastes of herbs and cherries.

Sangiovese also provides up to 80 percent of the Vino Nobile di Montepulciano blend, while under its pseudonym, Brunello, it is left unblended, making what is in effect a single varietal wine—Brunello di Montalcino, a big, dark wine with plenty of tannin.

As well as its role in such traditional Tuscan wines, Sangiovese is also an important component (along with Cabernet Sauvignon and Merlot) in making the more modern wines known as the "Super Tuscans". Owing to the fact that non-indigenous grapes are used, such wines remained unclassified for many years, until the authorities could ignore them no longer. They now enjoy their own classification with prices to match.

Sangiovese used to not be seen much outside Italy, but there are new plantings of the variety in Mendoza province in Argentina and it is becoming increasingly fashionable in California and Australia as producers experiment with new varieties.

STYLE

Medium to full-bodied fruity, classy Sangiovese should be soft and velvety and noted for its sour cherry aromas.

GOES WITH

Chianti is a good partner for most simple chicken dishes and, being Italian, it goes perfectly with pasta dishes and pizza.

FAMOUS SANGIOVESES

Sangiovese is the major grape behind such celebrated Italian wines as Chianti, Brunello di Montalcino, and Vino Nobile di Montepulciano.

STYLE

Fruity and spicy, but often also flabby and rubbery.

GOES WITH

Drink with braised dishes, roast meats, and richly sauced dishes.

FAMOUS PINOTAGES

Best examples come from Paarl and Stellenbosch.

PINOTAGE

Pinotage is regarded as South Africa's own grape variety, having been developed there in 1925 as a cross between Pinot Noir and Cinsault. Even the name Pinotage is a hybrid, being a cross between Pinot Noir and Hermitage, the South African name for Cinsault.

Its main home remains South Africa, although there are also plantings in California and scatterings elsewhere. Pinotage wines are invariably deep purple in color and are often characterized on the nose by remarkably unenticing whiffs of burnt rubber.

When it's as it should be, Pinotage can make wines of freshness and fruit, marked by raspberry-like flavors, but all too frequently it is one-dimensional and flat. Often tannic and chewy, Pinotage is sometimes compared to Syrah, although it lacks much of that grape's style and panache. Styles vary between fruity wines designed to be drunk young and full-bodied wines that need aging; either way, despite its qualities and its individuality, Pinotage remains an acquired taste.

ZINFANDEL

Zinfandel is known as California's own grape, being the region's only indigenous variety and it's widely planted. It is believed to be related to the little-known Primitivo grape found in Italy.

California remains Zinfandel's favored home, but it is being grown with increasing success in Australia, South America, and South Africa. Zinfandel produces wines similar to those of Cabernet Sauvignon, albeit with higher levels of alcohol and softer tannins, which may be drunk young or allowed to develop with age.

The range of wines produced by Zinfandel is bewildering: while it makes some of California's most respected and sought-after wines, full bodied and rich in alcohol, it also makes semi-sweet white wine, "blush" wine, jug wine, sparkling wine, and even fortified wine.

Most commercially successful are the so-called "white Zinfandels" (which are usually pink), blended wines which may include other grapes, too, such as the white variety Muscat. The resulting semi-sweet wines are the closest that anyone has come to creating alcoholic cotton candy in liquid form, and are best avoided.

STYLE

Red and full-bodied; pink and off-dry; fortified.

GOES WITH

Drink the big red versions with barbecued foods, chili con carne, or roast lamb.

FAMOUS ZINFANDELS

The indigenous grape of California.

BARBERA

Barbera makes solid, everyday wines that are purple-colored with good acidity and plenty of chewy, raisiny fruit. Barbera's wines need little time to mature and their low tannin levels ensure that they are invariably soft and smooth, and always a pleasure to drink, without reaching the heights enjoyed by its two big rivals Nebbiolo and Sangiovese.

Its main homes are Piedmont, Lombardy, and Emilia-Romagna in northern Italy and its best-known wines are Barbera d'Alba, Barbera d'Asti—both robust and full-bodied—and, in combination with other varieties, Barbera del Monferrato. Barbera is extremely versatile, capable of making rosés and sparkling wines, some of which can be sweet. Despite its undoubted qualities, its popularity is waning in Italy—and is giving way to other varieties.

Further away, in hotter regions, Barbera's high alcohol and good acidity levels make it an ideal variety for blending, and it appears in Argentina, California (where it is increasingly being planted in the San Joaquin Valley), former Yugoslavia, South America, and Australia.

NEBBIOLO

Italy's answer to Syrah, Nebbiolo makes the big, dark, tannic wines of Barolo and Barbaresco in the northwest region of Piedmont, its name deriving from the Nebbia, the fog which creeps over the Piedmontese hills.

Usually regarded as Italy's finest wines, Barolo and Barbaresco both spend regulated periods in oak barrels. Barolo is seen as the more robust and long-lived of these two massive wines, while Barbaresco is considered more elegant and refined: neither of them are cheap. Other wines made from the variety include Gattinara, Ghemme, and Spanna, usually being a blend of other varieties, too, making them gentler and more approachable than the big two.

The grape's wines are rich, full-bodied, chewy and tannic. Deep in color, the wines are intense and complex and often identifiable by their aromas of violets, raspberries, prunes, and chocolate. They usually require plenty of aging, although some producers are experimenting with modern-style wines, which require less maturation. Nebbiolo's wines are invariably high in alcohol, usually 13 percent or over: they are certainly neither for the faint-hearted nor the aperitif wine drinker. Although it can produce wines of striking intensity and is recognized as one of the world's finest varieties, Nebbiolo is scarcely grown anywhere other than in north-west Italy, although some enterprising wine makers are giving it a go in California.

STYLE

High in ripe currant fruit and acidity, low in tannin with elusive smokey aromas.

GOES WITH

Ideal with rich food with creamy sauces, or pasta and cold meats.

FAMOUS BARBARAS

Barbera d'Alba, Barbera d'Asti.

STYLE

Structured, powerful, alcoholic, and intense.

GOES WITH

Roast pork, oxtail stew, strong hard cheeses.

FAMOUS NEBBIOLOS

Barolo, Barbaresco, Gattinara, Ghemme, Spanna.

GAMAY

Although Beaujolais is Gamay's main home, the grape is also grown with considerable success in the Loire, where it makes wines such as Anjou Rosé, Anjou Gamay, and Gamay de Touraine. Switzerland, too, grows a considerable amount of Gamay, most frequently blending it with Pinot Noir. In the Mâconnais and the Côte Chalonnaise in Burgundy, Pinot Noir is also used as its blending partner in the easy-drinking Bourgogne Passe-Tout-Grains, adding body and depth.

Gamay makes light, fresh, and fruity red wines packed with the juicy flavors of peaches, cherries, and berries. Typically, its wines are high in acid, low in tannin, and sometimes lacking depth, but they are invariably easy-drinking wines and are among the few red wines which benefit from being lightly chilled.

Gamay is at its best when drunk young, and only the highest quality Beaujolais from fine years should be left to mature. Posters declaring that *Le Beaujolais Nouveau est arrivé* are a familiar wine bar sight every November when, on the third Thursday of the month, that year's vintage of Beaujolais—then barely two months old—is released for immediate consumption. In good vintages this is a charming frivolity to be enjoyed uncritically with friends: in bad vintages it is an acidic PR stunt best avoided.

STYLE

Vivid purple, juicy, and jammy.

GOES WITH

A red wine that benefits from being lightly chilled. Goes well with salads, cold meats, savory tarts, and even grilled tuna. Ideal for picnics.

FAMOUS GAMAYS

All red Beaujolais such as Brouilly, Chénas, Chiroubles, Côte de Brouilly, Fleurie, Juliénas, Morgon, Moulin à Vent, Régnié, and St. Amour.

MALBEC

Malbec ripens early and produces soft wines low in tannin and acidity which are marked by spicy, blackberry flavors. It was once an integral part of Bordeaux's blended clarets, but has fallen out of favor recently, often being regarded as no better than a poor man's Merlot. The only areas of Bordeaux that still regard it with any respect are Bourg and Blaye—where the vineyards are more or less divided equally between Malbec, Cabernet Sauvignon, and Merlot—and St. Emilion. Elsewhere in France, Malbec manages to cling on in the Loire where winemakers blend it with other varieties, such as Gamay and Cabernet Franc.

The variety is popular in the Americas. Producers in California continue to use Malbec in the old Bordeaux manner, blending it with the traditional varieties of Cabernet Sauvignon, Merlot, and Petit Verdot in their Meritage wines. It is grown with some success in Chile, while the wine makers of Argentina—where it is the third most planted variety are more adventurous, making highly successful single varietal wines from the grape. There are also plantings in New Zealand, notably in Hawkes Bay.

STYLE

Spicy, soft, deep-colored, and full of red berry flavors.

GOES WITH

Grilled steaks, barbecued ribs, or sausages and mashed potatoes.

FAMOUS MALBECS

Malbec is usually blended as part of the so-called "Black Wine" of Cahors (of which it usually comprises up to 70 percent) for example. But look out for the increasingly sophisticated single varietal Malbec from Argentina.

MOURVEDRE

Originally from Catalonia in Spain—where it is called Monastrell, Mourvèdre is now most associated with the south of France, where it plays its part in making the solid, fruity, everyday drinking wines of the region that are, as yet, rarely exported. In the Southern Rhône it is one of the region's most respected varieties, adding color, spice, and structure to Châteauneuf-du-Pape's blend.

Of the many southern French wines to which Mourvèdre adds its fresh fruit flavors, the best-known are Bandol (which must comprise at least 50 percent), Cassis, Corbières, Côtes du Roussillon, Côte du Rhône-Villages, and Palette. Although Mourvèdre is blended with Cinsault, Syrah, Carignan, or Grenache in most of these wines, it is also beginning to see a following as a single varietal in some of the newer Languedoc vineyards.

It is Spain's second most important black grape after Garnacha (Grenache), being well-suited to the warm climate and making the big, heavy reds and rosés of Valencia and Alicante. Also known as Mataro, Mourvèdre can be found in both Australia, where some interesting single varietal wines are being made, and in California. It is also used to make local wine in Algeria.

STYLE

Blackberry and licorice scented, peppery, chewy, and tannic.

GOES WITH

Full-flavored red meat or game.

FAMOUS MOURVEDRES

Boosts blends such as Corbières, Côtes de Provence, Côtes du Roussillon, Bandol.

CARIGNAN

Carignan originated in the Cariñena area of Aragon in northern Spain, where it continues to make fairly dreary full-bodied table wine. Although it is an integral part of the wines of Rioja, adding color to that region's wines, its main home in Spain is Catalonia, where it is also chiefly used for blending.

Being a late-ripener, Carignan does well in hot climates, and it has long dominated Languedoc-Roussillon, especially in Aude, Hérault, Gard, and Pyrénées-Orientales. These days, however, it is no longer in fashion and many of its vines are being uprooted and replanted with more popular varieties, although it is still, just, France's most widely grown red grape. Although most of its wines end up as simple *vin de table*, Carignan does play an important part in the blends that make up such well-regarded French country wines as Corbières, Fitou, Minervois, and the Provençal rosés. Its regular blending partners are Cinsault in the western Midi and Grenache in the eastern Midi.

Incredibly, Carignan was once the most widely grown variety in California, until a gum-chewing grape called Cabernet Sauvignon hit town.

STYLE

Dark, hefty wines that are high in both alcohol and tannin.

GOES WITH

Braised dishes and beef stews.

FAMOUS CARIGNANS

A component of Minervois, Corbières, Fitou, and many of Spain's Riojas.

CINSAULT

The fourth most planted variety in France, Cinsault is grown mainly in Languedoc-Roussillon where it is highly productive, making wines that are high in acidity and low in tannin. Cinsault is used chiefly in blends, providing smoothness, spice, perfume, and fruit, although some single varietal rosés are made, too. In Languedoc-Roussillon (notably in Aude, Hérault, and Gard) it is usually blended with Carignan or Grenache, and in the Southern Rhône—where it produces deeper-colored, more concentrated wines—it is frequently blended with Mourvèdre, Grenache, or Syrah. Used in Châteauneuf-du-Pape, Cinsault is also an obligatory ingredient in the basic Côtes du Rhône-Villages.

Its high productivity led Cinsault to be widely planted in South Africa where, for some reason, it is sometimes known as Hermitage. South Africa's own variety, called Pinotage, is a cross between Cinsault and Pinot Noir.

Cinsault is best blended with richer varieties such as Mourvèdre, Syrah, and, occasionally, Cabernet Sauvignon, a combination which has proved particularly successful in southern France, Australia, and Lebanon where, most famously, it is used at Château Musar.

STYLE
Perfumed, spicy, and pale-colored.

GOES WITH
Cinsault rosés are delicious on their own.

FAMOUS CINSAULTS
Used in Côtes du Rhône-Villages, Châteauneuf-du-Pape blends, and Lebanon's Ch. Musar.

PETIT VERDOT

Petit Verdot makes full-bodied wines, noted for their depth of color and spicy, peppery characteristics. It is a high-quality grape that is not dissimilar to Syrah in its deep color and peppery spiciness. Until recently, it was little seen, though, outside Bordeaux where it has long been used as a sort of vinous monosodium glutamate, adding a touch of zip to claret's triumvirate of Cabernet Sauvignon, Merlot, and Cabernet Franc by enhancing the blend's color, flavor, and tannin.

When used in such a fashion it usually comprises as little as 2–3 percent of the blend and certainly never more than 10 percent. It is used chiefly in the southern Médoc, where the soil produces light wines which are more in need of an extra dash of flavor than are the wines of the northern Médoc.

There has been a noticeable renaissance in the New World, though, for Petit Verdot, with major plantings in South America and California either for single varietal wines or to add oomph to blends.

STYLE
Deeply colored and full-flavored.

GOES WITH
Simple broiled meat dishes.

FAMOUS PETIT VERDOTS
It is still usually blended with other, classier grapes.

WHITE GRAPES

Over the following pages you will meet the most important white grapes—Chardonnay, Riesling, Sauvignon Blanc, and Sémillon—along with over a dozen other leading varieties.

The big four can be found all over the world, with Chardonnay in particular being famous—or notorious—for its ubiquity. But while the popularity of this quartet is constant, other varieties come and go with fashion. Viognier, for example, once restricted to a corner of the Rhône Valley, is now hugely popular with winemakers and consumers alike. While Pinot Gris is emerging from its Alsace heartland to gain a following further away. And as technology improves, so producers find it easier to plant and vinify those varieties that hitherto were too tricky to grow in marginal climes.

Once you can identify the different varieties and the wines that they make, you will discover the wines you like and the wines you don't, and you will be well on your way to becoming an expert. Further research—which, let's be frank, will require some dedicated sluicing and slurping—will help you determine which wines make the ideal partners for which foods. White wines can be bone dry or richly sweet; they can be light and refreshing or headily alcoholic and they can be still or sparkling.

CHARDONNAY

STYLE

Chardonnay styles range from green and steely in Chablis, to rich and buttery in Australia and California. In countries such as Austria, it is even used to make stunning botrytised sweet wines. In Champagne, it makes the world's finest sparkling wines, either blended with Pinot Noir and Pinot Meunier or unblended as a Blanc de Blancs.

GOES WITH

Chablis goes well with shellfish, and white burgundy with chicken dishes and simple broiled fish. New World Chardonnays are ideal with rich and creamy fish dishes and even roast duck.

FAMOUS CHARDONNAYS

Meursault, Chassagne-Montrachet, Puligny-Montrachet, and Corton-Charlemagne.

The world's most popular grape variety? Definitely. When it's as it should be, Chardonnay's hard to beat.

Chardonnay is easy to grow, has good acid levels, high alcohol, ages well, blends happily with other varieties, and winemakers and wine drinkers can't get enough of it. It is rare to find a bad Chardonnay because it is difficult to make a poor wine from it. Chardonnay is responsible for champagne and Chablis, and for such well-known white burgundies as Meursault, Puligny-Montrachet, Corton-Charlemagne, and Pouilly-Fuissé. Chardonnay can taste very different depending upon where it is grown because of variations in climate and winemakers' techniques. For example, Chardonnays from Burgundy tend to be more

elegant and fresh compared to the bigger, more obvious styles in Australia or California, where warmer climates result in riper grapes. But even in two neighboring areas there can be pronounced differences, for while white burgundies can be nutty or toasty. The wines of nearby Chablis can be steely and flinty. Chardonnay does spectacularly well in Australia, New Zealand, South Africa, South America, Italy, and Spain. It is especially beloved by Californians, in whose state it is the most planted grape variety. In fact, to many Americans the word Chardonnay is synonymous with white wine, so widespread is the variety. But despite these major successes elsewhere, Burgundy remains its spiritual home.

One cannot speak of Chardonnay without mentioning oak, with which it has a special relationship. Oak barrels draw out Chardonnay's best characteristics, and give the wine aromas of vanilla, toast, and nuts. Oaked and unoaked can be very different: try both.

STYLE

In the Loire Valley the grape produces lean, restrained, and austere wines of great elegance, while in New Zealand it is more zesty and exuberant, boasting aromas of cut grass, asparagus, and gooseberry.

GOES WITH

All fish dishes, seafood, and light meals such as chicken salad. Also makes a fine aperitif.

FAMOUS SAUVIGNON BLANCS

Pouilly-Fumé, Sancerre. In the New World, most notable in New Zealand and Chile; also good from cooler areas of South Africa, California, and Australia. A vital ingredient in the sweet wines of Sauternes and Barsac.

SAUVIGNON BLANC

Sauvignon Blanc is one of the world's major grape varieties, celebrated as much for its distinctive, steely dry single varietals as it is for the role it plays in the world's finest dessert wines.

Sauvignon Blanc tends to prefer cool climate areas, and in France, the most celebrated examples are Sancerre and Pouilly-Fumé from the Loire, where producers don't believe in blending the variety, which they often call Blanc Fumé. Instead they prefer to make single varietal wines, which are fermented and aged in stainless steel vats rather than oak, creating wines that are crisp and clean-flavored with a smoky, mineral quality. Other lesser-known but good value Loire wines made from Sauvignon Blanc include Ménétou-Salon, Quincy, Reuilly, and Sauvignon de Touraine.

Sauvignon Blanc is crisper than Chardonnay and, to some, this is preferable to the soft butteriness of Chardonnay. Sauvignon is notable for its aromas of freshly cut grass, black currant leaves, gooseberries, asparagus, and, remarkably, but undeniably, cat's pee.

Impressive as it is on its own, arguably it is only when combined with Sémillon that Sauvignon Blanc achieves true greatness. In Bordeaux the dry wines of Entre-Deux-Mers and Graves are blends of Sauvignon Blanc and Sémillon (usually aged in oak), as are the great dessert wines of Sauternes and Barsac, and the lesser ones of St. Croix du Mont and Monbazillac.

Stunning Sauvignon Blancs come from New Zealand, where the wines of Sancerre and Pouilly-Fumé are given an extremely close run for their money. In California, too, it flourishes thanks to Robert Mondavi, who first pioneered the variety, terming it Fumé Blanc, and it is now second in popularity to Chardonnay, producing wines that tend to be less grassy than those of New Zealand or the Loire. The grape is also a great success in Chile and South Africa.

Apart from the sweet wines and fuller dry wines of Bordeaux, most Sauvignon Blancs are best drunk young—within three or four years of the vintage is a good guide.

SEMILLON

STYLE

Full-bodied wines of deep yellow, that can be dry or, when attacked by botrytis or late-picked, sumptuously sweet.

GOES WITH

Dry single varietal Sémillon goes well with smoked fish, such as trout, haddock, or mackerel. When sweet it goes beautifully with rich pâtés or with puddings such as *tarte tatin*.

FAMOUS SEMILLONS

Dry single varietals in Australia's Hunter Valley or, blended with Sauvignon Blanc, sweet wines in Sauternes and Barsac. Ch. Climens is a rare example of an unblended botrytis-affected Sémillon in Barsac.

Sémillon produces deep yellow wines that are full-bodied, high in both alcohol and aroma, low in acid, and age extremely well, being especially well-suited to oak.

It is one of the great unsung grapes of the world, and many people consume it without ever having heard of it, most notably in the wines of Bordeaux, where Sémillon adds roundness to the dry wines of Graves and the sweet ones of Sauternes and Barsac. It has recently become more prominent thanks to its role in blended wines from the New World, most of which are labeled varietally.

Unblended, Sémillon is apt to make undistinguished, forgettable wines, but when it is combined with Sauvignon Blanc, great things happen. Sauvignon Blanc provides the acidity and aromas while Sémillon softens Sauvignon Blanc's rougher edges to make sublime wines which are often greater than either variety can make on its own.

Sémillon is susceptible to noble rot and provides the lion's share of the blends that go to make up the finest Sauternes and Barsacs, whose rich, intensely honeyed and utterly delicious wines usually include about 80 percent Sémillon, 20 percent Sauvignon Blanc, and a slurp of Muscadelle.

Australia, where Sémillon drops the acute accent and is sometimes called Hunter Valley Riesling, makes some fine single varietals, mainly in New South Wales and the Hunter Valley, perhaps proving to the doubters that the grape can stand alone. It is also blended very successfully with Chardonnay and makes fine dessert wines. Single varietal Sémillons are also made in South Africa, mainly in Paarl, Wellington, and the Franschhoek Valley, and in Chile, where it provides two-thirds of all white wine produced, much of it pretty basic—the grape tending to be fat and oily—and little of which is exported.

RIESLING

True Riesling is the most elegant of grapes and is most at home in Germany, where all the top wines, be they sweet or dry, are Rieslings.

The sweet wines are either late-picked or affected by noble rot and range in style from semi-sweet Spätlese through Auslese and Beerenauslese to sumptuously sweet Trocken-beerenauslese. Dry German Rieslings are crisp, lively, tangy, and refreshing, they are often light in alcohol and age remarkably well, gaining rich honey flavors as they do so. There are many inferior varieties that go under the name of Riesling, none of which have anything to do with the true Riesling. In California, the true Riesling is called Johannisberg Riesling, in Australia, it is known as Rhine Riesling, and in South Africa, as Weisser Riesling.

Remarkably, considering that it is regarded as one of the world's finest grapes—if not the finest—you won't find Riesling in France, other than in that schizophrenic part of the country, Alsace. Here it is considered top dog and makes fresh, lively wines, which, while delicate, are fuller and higher in alcohol than those from neighboring Germany.

The grape is also widely grown in Austria making dry, concentrated wines, and in Italy's Friuli and Alto Adige, where it makes light, elegant, and aromatic wines.

New Zealand grows Riesling in Marlborough, producing wines of excellent acidity and delicacy, and it features in Argentina and in Chile. Most of California is too warm to produce dry Riesling—the drinking public seems only to want Chardonnay anyway—but both Washington State and Ontario in Canada make use of the grape's preference for cool conditions to make wines of great delicacy. Australia's Rhine Rieslings, especially those from the Eden and Clare Valleys, are hugely sought after and greatly respected.

STYLE

Riesling is capable of making spare, austere, and elegant dry wines, rich, honeyed, and luscious sweet wines and even light, aromatic, and refreshing sparklers. The grape should be instantly identifiable in the glass, marked out by its distinctive aromas of gasoline, peaches, melons, apples, and limes.

GOES WITH

Drier German Rieslings go well with Pacific Rim cooking and other spicy food, while the sweet ones are perfect with fruit, nuts, or desserts.

FAMOUS RIESLINGS

Nearly all the white wines of Germany, and certainly all the great ones, are made from Riesling.

CHENIN BLANC

This grape comes originally from the Loire Valley in France where it is often known as Pineau de la Loire, and where its versatility is much in evidence: it is here that it produces such wines as the dry Savennières from Anjou, the dry, the sparkling, or the sweet Vouvrays from Touraine, the sweet late harvest Côteaux du Layons, and the sparkling wines of Saumur.

Gallons of indifferent and sharp table wine are made from Chenin Blanc in the Loire, too, which do not show the grape at its best.

Its susceptibility to botrytis, the noble rot that concentrates the sugar in the grape, makes it ideal for producing dessert wines, the best of which can last for decades, gaining beautiful golden hues and rich honey flavors as they age. Chenin Blanc's high natural acidity is perfect for making sparkling wine and it is an important component in the world's oldest sparkling wine, Blanquette de Limoux from the Midi.

Chenin Blanc thrives best in marginal climates and it is grown successfully in New Zealand and in South Africa, where it is the country's most popular variety, making light, dry, and refreshing wines. Elsewhere in the New World, Chenin Blanc is rarely accorded the respect that it receives in the Loire or South Africa. In Australia it is used mainly for blending into commercial wines while in California the clamor for Chardonnay and Sauvignon Blanc means that there is currently little consumer interest in it.

STYLE

Chenin Blanc is an extraordinary grape that can produce still and sparkling wine, sweet and dry wine, fortified wine, and liquor.

GOES WITH

Nothing goes better with strawberries and cream or a fruit tart than a sweet Vouvray.

FAMOUS CHENIN BLANCS

Vouvray, Savennières, Coteaux du Layon.

GEWURZTRAMINER

Gewurztraminer may be the hardest variety to spell and to pronounce (nowadays it is generally spelled without the umlaut), but its deep golden color and exotic and heady aromas of lychees, spice, flowers, peaches, and apricots are unforgettable, making it a cinch to spot at blind tastings.

Although it is grown throughout Europe and is supposed to have originated in Italy's Alto Adige (where it is still known as Traminer Aromatico), Gewurztraminer is most at home in Alsace. Here the variety is at its most pungent, making sweet-smelling but intensely dry wines, high in alcohol, low in acidity, and bursting with spicy flavors. In great years, rich and honeyed late harvest wines, known as Vendanges Tardives, are made as, too, in exceptional years, are botrytis-affected wines known as Sélection de Grains Nobles.

Gewürz is the German word for spice, and Gewurztraminer is highly regarded both in Germany, especially in the Pfalz just over the border from Alsace, and in Austria. The grape does best in cool climates, and in the New World it is happiest in New Zealand, although there are some plantings in Australia, too. In California it is grown only in the cooler areas such as Carneros, Anderson Valley, Monterey County, and Mendocino, where it makes scented wines, noticeably softer and less spicy than those of Alsace. Some wines are also being made successfully in Oregon in America's Pacific Northwest.

STYLE

Can be sweet or dry and is characterized by a heady aroma of lychees.

GOES WITH

Great with spicy food.

FAMOUS GEWURZTRAMINERS

Alsace is its spiritual home.

GOES WITH

Great with fish pâté, seafood
pasta, and salads.

FAMOUS PINOT
BLANCS

Pinot Blanc is best known
in Alsace.

STYLE

Can be crisp and dry, or full,
smoky, and honeyed

GOES WITH

Being low in acid, Pinot Gris
goes especially well with food.

FAMOUS PINOT GRIS

Alsace Tokay-Pinot Gris, Italian
Pinot Grigio.

PINOT BLANC

Pinot Blanc is not dissimilar to Chardonnay, to which it was once thought to be related, although it is not nearly so complex, flavorsome, or sophisticated. At its best it should be fresh, lively, and appealing with flavors of yeast and apples, backed up by the faintest hints of honey. But although it is invariably light and pleasing on the palate, it never really seems to have a great deal to say. Its high acidity makes it ideal for making sparkling wines and it is used as the base for most of Alsace's fizzy Crémant d'Alsace.

Pinot Blanc also makes drinkable, if undramatic, dry white wines in Alsace, the lightest of the region which, while well-regarded, are usually eclipsed by those of Pinot Gris. It is grown throughout Italy—where it is called Pinot Bianco—notably in the Veneto, Alto Adige, and Lombardy where it makes pleasant sparkling wine, and is an important part of the blend that makes Soave.

As Weissburgunder, Pinot Blanc is increasingly popular in Germany, making both dry and sweet wines—especially in Baden and the Pfalz—and it is grown throughout Austria, even being used to make botrytized Trockenbeerenauslese.

PINOT GRIS

Pinot Gris produces fragrant white wines of depth and substance, with styles ranging from crisp, light, and dry, to rich, full, and honeyed. At its best it makes a fine alternative to white burgundy and can be full-bodied enough to drink with dishes that are more usually accompanied by red wines. Although technically a white grape, Pinot Gris is a mutation of the red Pinot Noir and it can produce wines that are almost rosé in color.

Pinot Gris thrives in Alsace (where it is sometimes still known as Tokay d'Alsace or Tokay-Pinot Gris), not only producing big, smoky, dry wines but also the remarkably intense Vendanges Tardives. Around Touraine, in the Loire, it makes charming rosés, and in Switzerland's Valais it results in rich, full wines. While Pinot Gris is oily and fat in Alsace, it is lighter, spritzier, and more acidic in Italy, where—known as Pinot Grigio—it is grown mainly in Friuli, Lombardy, and in small areas of Emilia-Romagna. Germany grows more Pinot Gris—known there as Ruländer—than any other country, producing juicy wines of low acidity and spicy aroma most especially in Württemberg, Baden, and The Pfalz. It is starting to catch on in the New World, and is increasing in popularity in California, especially amongst those bored by the ubiquity of Chardonnay.

MUSCAT

Muscat is thought to be the oldest grape variety known to man, its hundreds of different incarnations producing many styles of wine. It may sound odd, but Muscat is the only grape to produce wine that actually tastes and smells of grapes—indeed, Muscat is probably the only winemaking grape to produce delicious table grapes.

One of the grape's best-known strains, Muscat Blanc à Petits Grains, is responsible for the fortified Muscat de Beaumes-de-Venise from the Southern Rhône and, blended with Clairette, the sparkling Clairette de Die in the Northern Rhône. In Italy it is the flavor behind Asti Spumante, and in Greece it makes the dessert wines of Samos, Pátras, and Cephalonia. In Australia, known as Brown Muscat or Frontignan, it makes delicious fortified liqueur wines, as it does in California, where it is known as Muscat Blanc, Muscat Canelli, or Muscat Frontignan.

Muscat Ottonel is grown in Alsace for heady dry wines and in Austria for sublime dessert wines. Muscat of Alexandria is usually used for table grapes, but in Spain it is used to make the heavy, sweet, fortified wine, Moscatel de Málaga and, in Portugal, Moscatel de Setúbal.

Orange Muscat and Muscat Hamburg are grown in Australia and California for dessert wine, the latter, known as Black Muscat, only rarely being used.

SILVANER

Silvaner originated in Austria, in which country it still thrives, albeit less ubiquitously than before. Despite being edged out by its own ungrateful offspring—Müller-Thurgau (a cross between Riesling and Silvaner)—as the country's most planted variety, it is still much grown in Germany, mainly in the Rheinhessen, the Pfalz, and Franken, in which latter region, where Riesling is difficult to ripen, it does especially well.

In France, Sylvaner is virtually unknown outside Alsace where it makes easy-drinking, rather nondescript wines at the lower end of the price range. Even here it is planted with much less frequency than before. Switzerland remains true to the variety, especially in the Valais where it is known as Johannisberg, making drinkable, refreshing wines of no great character. It used to be grown fairly widely in California, but in the charge to plant Sauvignon Blanc and Chardonnay, it has all but been forgotten.

STYLE

Can be sweet or dry but always aromatic. Smells of grapes.

GOES WITH

When sweet, perfect with desserts or blue cheeses.

FAMOUS MUSCAT

Muscat de Beaumes-de-Venise.

STYLE

Light and drinkable.

GOES WITH

Sylvaner from Alsace goes well with onion tarts and quiches, and is delicious with bouillabaisse.

FAMOUS SYLVANER

Best in Germany, Austria, and Alsace.

ALIGOTE

STYLE

Zesty and dry.

GOES WITH

Best drunk as an aperitif, either on its own, or with a dash of crème de cassis as a kir.

FAMOUS ALIGOTES

Bourgogne Aligoté.

Aligoté is little seen outside Burgundy, where it languishes in the shadow of Chardonnay, and even in Burgundy its popularity is waning. It is grown mainly in the Mâconnais and Côte Chalonnaise, areas where it makes zesty dry white wine, which is usually labeled Bourgogne Aligoté. At its best its wines can be soft and creamy with hints of citrus, but all too often it is acidic and short-lived.

In Burgundy, Aligoté is habitually used for making kir, a traditional drink in which the wine's acidity is softened by a dash of crème de cassis. It says a lot about a wine that even the locals would rather not drink it unless it is adulterated with black currant liqueur. Nonetheless, the variety remains popular in Eastern Europe, especially Georgia, where it is often used to make sparkling wine.

VIOGNIER

Viognier is suddenly a rather fashionable variety with both growers and drinkers alike, having gained its reputation by producing the extraordinarily intense dry white wines from the tiny vineyards of Château Grillet and Condrieu next door to Côte Rôtie in the Northern Rhône. Restaurants which had never heard of Viognier ten years ago, now stock several examples of the variety, which are well worth seeking out although the best are likely to be pricey.

Good Viogniers are big-boned beauties with alluring, but fleeting, scents of peaches and apricots, comparable in their headiness of aroma and pungency of flavor with Gewurztraminer. The less good examples, however, can be overpowering and lacking in finesse.

STYLE

Aromatic and concentrated.

GOES WITH

The perfect foil for grilled or pâté de foie gras.

FAMOUS VIOGNIERS

Condrieu and Ch. Grillet.

Viognier is something of a curiosity in that it has long been used as an aromatic addition to the great red wines of Côte Rôtie, being vinified alongside the red grape Syrah and permitted to comprise up to 20 percent of the final blend.

It is being seen more often in Italy and Australia as well as in other parts of France, such as Languedoc-Roussillon, where some notable single varietals are being produced and marketed under the name of the variety rather than the wines' geographic locations. Viognier is also currently the flavor of the month in California but, despite its current popularity, the grape remains a rarity with very few plantings, and with some producers questioning whether or not investing in a potential passing fad is worth struggling with the grape's low productivity and its susceptibility to disease.

MULLER-THURGAU

Müller-Thurgau is a hybrid variety created in 1882 by Dr. Hermann Müller, from the Swiss canton of Thurgau, who, in crossing Riesling with Silvaner, hoped to combine the quality of the former with the early-ripening capability of the latter. At its best, its wines are light, fresh, fruity, and fragrant; at worst they are bland, characterless, and utterly lacking in flavor.

Müller-Thurgau is the most planted variety in Germany making the infamous bottled bubblegum, Liebfraumilch wine. The grape ripens almost anywhere, producing enormous amounts of extremely dull, medium-dry, and some sweet, wine. The grape has a tendency to be a bit mousy in Germany though, and makes cleaner and fresher wines in Italy's Alto Adige, Luxembourg, and in England, where it is also the most planted variety.

The grape was the mainstay of New Zealand's embryonic wine industry, producers believing it to be the variety best suited to their climate, and indeed it probably makes better wine there than it does anywhere else. However, as the industry has grown and as tastes have become more sophisticated, so Chardonnay and Sauvignon Blanc have far outstripped Müller-Thurgau in terms of popularity.

STYLE

Fruity and off-dry.

GOES WITH

Müller-Thurgau should be drunk on its own or with light, delicately flavored dishes.

FAMOUS MULLER-THURGAUS

Best-known for its Liebfraumilch, unfortunately, but some delicately fruity and refreshing examples can be found.

COLOMBARD

Colombard originated in the Charente region of France and it was used originally for distillation into Cognac and Armagnac. It has been largely supplanted in this role by Ugni Blanc, as Trebbiano is known there, and so growers have turned to making it into simple, undemanding wines such as Vin de Pays des Côtes de Gascogne—crisp and spicy off-dry wines of high acidity and flowery perfume.

Remarkably, this productive, but little-known, variety is now one of the most widely planted varieties in California where—called French Colombard—it is prized for its ability to produce simple crisp wines in a warm climate. For similar reasons it is also extensively grown in both Australia and South Africa, where it is often blended with Chenin Blanc to make everyday drinking wines or sparklers.

STYLE

Light, fruity, and refreshing.

GOES WITH

Ideal for knocking back, well-chilled, at picnics or outdoors on late summer evenings.

FAMOUS COLOMBARDS

Vin de Pays des Côtes de Gascogne.

ROUSSANNE

Roussanne is the more refined half of the celebrated Roussanne/Marsanne double act. In the Northern Rhône in particular the two grapes are inextricably linked, joining forces to produce the white versions of Hermitage, Crozes-Hermitage, and St. Joseph, as well as being used in small amounts in the red Hermitage blend, adding softness to the otherwise unblended Syrah. Roussanne is less widely grown than Marsanne, not least because it is prone to powdery mildew and rot and has an irregular yield, but it is the more stylish and polished of the two, and its wines age more gracefully. In the Southern Rhône, it is used in the blends that make both the red and the white Châteauneuf-du-Pape.

Roussanne is also grown in Languedoc-Roussillon, where the warm climate ensures that its tendency to ripen late is less of a problem than it is in the Northern Rhône, or in Savoie in eastern France, where small amounts of single varietal Roussanne can be found if you can be bothered to look hard enough.

Roussanne has a spicier flavor than Marsanne, and while its wines are delicious when young, with a tendency to blossom in later years, they can, like those of Marsanne, be a bit grumpy in middle age. The two grapes also combine to make the Rhône's *méthode traditionelle* wine, St. Péray, a full-flavored sparkler with an almost nutty taste.

STYLE

Spicy and full-bodied.

GOES WITH

White Rhônes go with smoked eel and salmon, and gravadlax.

FAMOUS ROUSSANNES

White Hermitage and Crozes-Hermitage (blended with Marsanne).

MARSANNE

Marsanne is a vigorous grape which produces deep-colored, brown-tinged wine high in alcohol with a distinctive and heady aroma reminiscent of apples, pears, glue, nuts, spice, and almonds. The grape's full flavor, coupled with a low acidity, means that it is ideal for blending, and the variety with which it is invariably linked is Roussanne, which plays Tweedledum to Marsanne's Tweedledee. It is a highly successful partnership, responsible for such white wines of the Northern Rhône as Côtes du Rhône-Blanc, Crozes-Hermitage, Hermitage, and St. Joseph. Marsanne is also one of the grapes permitted in the blend which makes the Southern Rhône's comparatively rare white Châteauneuf-du-Pape.

Although Marsanne is traditionally seen as making long-lived, full-bodied wines that sometimes can be dull when young, modern winemaking techniques are changing such perceptions, and fruity, perfumed wines are being produced for early consumption. When young, its wines are now flowery and aromatic, when old they are rich and nutty; indeed, it seems nowadays that only in its middle-age is it dull. Increasingly grown in the Midi, Marsanne makes fleshy white wines in Cassis, and the dry, sweet, still and sparkling wines of St. Péray, south of Cornas in the Northern Rhône. It is a permitted ingredient in the Northern Rhône's Syrah-dominated red Hermitage, and is grown successfully in the Valais, in Switzerland, where it is known as Ermitage Blanc.

As for the New World, Marsanne has been grown in Victoria in Australia since the 1860s making big, long-lived wines, but it is seen only occasionally in California where it appears as either single varietals or blended with its old Rhône chum Roussanne.

STYLE
Full-flavored and heady.

GOES WITH
A fine white Rhône is perfect with heavily sauced lobster dishes.

FAMOUS MARSANNES
White Hermitage and Crozes-Hermitage (blended with Roussanne). Marsanne from Victoria, Australia.

TREBBIANO

No grape produces more of the world's wine than Trebbiano, and it remains the most widely planted variety in France, where it is known as Ugni Blanc. The grape is notorious for producing bland, nondescript wines of little character, and so, on the principle that the worse the base wine the better the brandy—much of it is used for distillation.

In Italy it appears blended with other varieties in such wines as Est! Est!! Est!!!, Frascati, Orvieto, Soave, Verdicchio, and Vernaccia di San Gimignano; it even finds its way into red Chianti.

Trebbiano is also grown in California—mainly in the San Joaquin Valley—and in Mexico, in both cases chiefly being used for distillation.

STYLE
Bland and undemanding.

GOES WITH
Fritto misto on the quayside of an Italian fishing village.

FAMOUS TREBBIANOS
In Italian blends such as Soave, Frascati, Verdicchio.

KEY AREAS

The world is producing more wine

than ever before from many more countries,

and while the Old World continues

to delight, there is much to tempt the

wine lover in the New.

FRANCE

CHAMPAGNE

Seine

Paris

ALSACE

LOIRE VALLEY

Loire

CHABLIS

Dijon

BURGUNDY

JURA

SAVOIE

Lyon

BORDEAUX

Bordeaux

Dordogne

RHONE
VALLEY

SOUTH-WEST
FRANCE

Garonne

LANGUEDOC-
ROUSSILLON

PROVENCE

Marseille

France may not boast the most vineyards
in the world (that honor goes to Spain),
but it is still the daddy, touching heights
that other countries can only dream about.

WINES TO LOOK FOR

Clarets, dry whites, and intensely sweet dessert wines.

TIP

If you find that one of the great names of Bordeaux is beyond you financially (and they are beyond most of us financially) look out for the château's second label.

BORDEAUX

Bordeaux remains the most celebrated wine region of them all, capable of producing exquisite wines which, once tasted, are never forgotten.

The vast majority of its wines are red, known in the UK as "claret." Some remarkable sweet wines are also produced, and some fine dry whites.

The region lies in the southwest of France, near the Atlantic coast, straddling the River Gironde that later splits into the Rivers Garonne and Dordogne. On the so-called Left Bank is the Médoc, and such wine-growing communes as St. Estèphe, Pauillac, St. Julien, Margaux, Pessac-Léognan, Barsac, and Sauternes. On the Right Bank are the areas of Fronsac, Canon-Fronsac, Pomerol, and St. Emilion. The tongue of land between the two rivers is known as the Entre-Deux-Mers.

Cabernet Sauvignon is the dominant red grape, except chiefly in St. Emilion and Pomerol, where conditions favor Merlot. Sauvignon Blanc and Sémillon are responsible for both the dry whites and the sweet dessert wines (where the grapes are affected by noble rot or botrytis). Less powerful sweet wines can be found in Ste-Croix-du-Mont near the town of Langon.

Nearly all the wine-growing properties in Bordeaux are called Château Something-or-Other, and while this doesn't mean that there is a grand house at every vineyard, some of the châteaux are indeed extremely grand. In 1855, the top châteaux of the Médoc (and one from Péssac-Léognan —Ch. Haut-Brion) were classified into five divisions known as Crus Classés, ranging from Premier Cru Classé (First Growth) down to Cinquième Cru Classé (Fifth Growth). This original classification was established solely on price and there are those who believe it now to be outdated, but it does give some idea of quality. Below the Crus Classés are Crus Bourgeois, below which come Bordeaux Supérieur and straight Bordeaux.

Just to make things even more complicated, the wines of Graves (the top estates of which are now classified as Pessac-Léognan) and St. Emilion were divided into two ranks in 1953 and 1955 respectively. There is one category, Cru Classé, in the former region and two, Premier Grand Cru Classé and Grand Cru Classé, in the latter.

MAJOR RED GRAPES

Cabernet Sauvignon, Merlot, Cabernet Franc, Malbec, Petit Verdot.

MAJOR WHITE GRAPES

Sémillon, Sauvignon Blanc, Muscadelle.

KEY PRODUCERS

Ch. Haut-Brion, Ch. Lafite-Rothschild, Ch. Latour, Ch. Margaux, Ch. Mouton-Rothschild, Ch. Palmer, Ch. Le Pin, Ch. Cheval Blanc, Ch. Léoville-Barton, Ch. Gruaud-Larose, Ch. Pétrus, and Ch. d'Yquem.

FINE VINTAGES

Red: 1990, 1994, 1995, 1996, 1998, 1999, 2000, 2001, 2002, 2003.
White: 1990, 1995, 1996, 1997, 1998, 1999, 2001, 2003.

MAJOR GRAPES

Chardonnay, Pinot Noir, and,
in Beaujolais, Gamay.

KEY PRODUCERS

BURGUNDY (NEGOCIANTS):
Joseph Drouhin,
J. Faiveley, Louis Jadot,
Louis Latour.
BURGUNDY (DOMAINES): Domaine
Romanée Conti, Grivot,
Leflaive, Bonneau du Martray,
Rosseau, Lafon.
CHABLIS: Daniel-Etienne Defaix,
Jean-Marc Brocard, Raveneau,
William Fèvre, Billaud-Simon.
BEAUJOLAIS: Georges Duboeuf,
Chauvet, Charvet, Tête,
Chignard.

WINES TO LOOK FOR

Red: Gevrey-Chambertin,
Corton, Pernand-Vergelesses,
Pommard, Vosne-Romanée,
White: Corton-Charlemagne,
Puligny-Montrachet, Chassagne-
Montrachet, Pouilly-Fuissé.

BURGUNDY & CHABLIS

In one sense, Burgundy is the easiest of all French
wine regions to get to grips with, and in another sense
it is the hardest.

It is the easiest because there are no complicated combinations of grape varieties to remember. Bar a few quirky rarities, all the wines from the region are what are now known as single varietals: all red burgundies are made from Pinot Noir and all white burgundies and Chablis are made from Chardonnay. The only other grape to remember is Gamay from which all Beaujolais is made. It is the hardest region to understand because the wines are named after the villages where the grapes are grown (rather than single estates as in Bordeaux), with the vineyards therein possibly having several hundred different owners, with some possessing little more than a row or two each. The wine that each of these growers makes— or sells to larger *négociants*—varies dramatically.

Burgundy runs roughly north to south between Dijon and Lyon, with Chablis—home to some of the finest Chardonnays in the world and categorized in four quality levels descending from Chablis Grand Cru, Chablis Premier Cru, Chablis, to Petit Chablis—out on a limb up near Auxerre, north west of Dijon. The heart of the region, the Côte d'Or, is made up of the Côte de Nuits, which is home to long-lasting red wines such as Gevrey-Chambertin, Nuits-St-Georges, and Vosne-Romanée, and the Côte de Beaune, source of top-class reds such as Beaune, Pommard, Volnay, and Aloxe-Corton, and iconic whites such as Meursault, Puligny-Montrachet, and Corton-Charlemagne. Further south is the Côte Chalonnaise, which boasts reds such as Givry and Mercurey, and whites such as Montagny, and the Mâconnais, known for its good-quality whites like Pouilly-Fuissé, St. Véran, and Mâcon-Lugny. Beaujolais lies at the end of this irregular line and is made up of such villages (and wines) as Brouilly, Morgon, Chiroubles, and St. Amour.

VINTAGES

Red: 1990, 1991, 1993, 1994, 1995, 1996, 1997, 1998, 1999, 2000, 2001, 2002, 2003.
White: 1990, 1992, 1993, 1994, 1995, 1996, 1997, 1998, 1999, 2000, 2001, 2002, 2003.
Chablis: 1990, 1992, 1995, 1996, 1997, 2000, 2002.

TIP

Getting to grips with Burgundy is a life's work. Once you find a producer/*négociant* you like, stick to them like glue.

THE RHONE

The Rhône, one of the great wine regions of the world, has been producing wine since the Romans were there.

The area, which runs south along the Rhône Valley from just below Lyon to Avignon, has become fashionable again among wine drinkers after far too long in the shadow of Bordeaux and Burgundy. Reds, whites, rosés, sparklers, sweet, and fortified wines are all made here, but it is chiefly for its mighty, long-lived red wines that the Rhône is renowned.

As far as wine drinkers are concerned, the region is divided between the Northern Rhône—home to such wines as Hermitage, Crozes-Hermitage, Côte Rôtie, and Cornas— and the Southern Rhône—famous for its Châteauneuf-du-Pape, Gigondas, and Vacqueyras. Generally speaking many more wines are made in the Southern Rhône than in the North but fewer great ones.

The two main red grapes are Syrah in the north and Grenache in the south, but although these two varieties dominate, many others are grown too, with a whopping 13 different grape varieties allowed in the wines of Châteauneuf-du-Pape. The main white grapes are Marsanne and Roussanne (both of which are permitted in the red wines of Hermitage, curiously enough) and Viognier, which is not only used in small amounts to soften the red wines of Côte Rôtie, but also to make the beguiling and spicy white wines of Condrieu.

The top quality reds are big, beefy wines with plenty of rich, ripe fruit and no shortage of tannin, with the Southern Rhône wines tending to be headier and more alcoholic than those of the North, but perhaps slightly softer.

In the Southern Rhône there are some pretty decent rosés to look out for such as those from Lirac and Tavel as well as the ridiculously addictive, lightly fortified sweet wines made from Muscat, known as Vins Doux Naturels, such as Muscat de Beaumes-de-Venise. Less interesting, but much more plentiful, are the more basic wines of the region such as Côtes du Rhône, Côtes-du-Rhône-Villages, Côtes du Ventoux, and Coteaux du Tricastin.

OPPOSITE, ABOVE AND BELOW LEFT
M. CHAPOUTIER, TAIN L'HERMITAGE
OPPOSITE, BELOW RIGHT
CHATEAUNEUF-DU-PAPE, RHONE VALLEY.

MAJOR RED GRAPES

Syrah and Grenache.

MAJOR WHITE GRAPES

Viognier, Marsanne, Roussanne.

KEY PRODUCERS

North: Chapoutier, Guigal, Paul Jaboulet-Aîné, Clape, Champet, Vidal-Fleury, Chave, Grippat.
South: Ch. de Beaucastel, H. Bonneau, Clos des Papes, Domaine du Vieux Télégraph, Domaine Rabasse-Charavin.

WINES TO LOOK FOR

North: Cornas, Côte Rôtie, Hermitage.
South: Châteauneuf-du-Pape, Gigondas, Vacqueyras.

FINE VINTAGES

1990, 1995, 1996, 1997, 1998, 1999, 2000, 2001, 2002, 2003.

TIP

Top class Rhônes age beautifully and can be great value.

MAJOR RED GRAPES

Pinot Noir, Pinot Meunier.

MAJOR WHITE GRAPES

Chardonnay.

KEY PRODUCERS

Billecart-Salmon, Bollinger, Duval-Leroy, Nicolas Feuillatte, Gosset, Krug, Lanson, Laurent-Perrier, Moët & Chandon, Mumm, Perrier-Jouët, Pol Roger, Pommery, Louis Roederer, Ruinart, Salon, Taittinger, Veuve Clicquot.

WINES TO LOOK FOR

Most of the production is devoted to nonvintage (NV) champagne—wines from different vintages blended to ensure consistency in each producer's distinctive house style.

CHAMPAGNE

The vineyards of Champagne, which are situated in the valley of the River Marne some 75 miles from Paris, are the most northerly in France.

The three principal wine-growing areas are La Grande Montagne de Reims, located south and southeast of the town of Reims; La Vallée de la Marne, near the town of Epernay, and La Côte des Blancs, south of Epernay. Poor quality soil—thin clay and a chalky sub-soil—and a difficult climate plagued by late frosts and hail storms, somehow combine to produce the most magical of all sparkling wines.

Only Chardonnay, Pinot Noir, and Pinot Meunier grapes may be used in the production of champagne. The grapes are picked and pressed, and the resulting juice undergoes an initial fermentation—usually in stainless steel tanks, although some traditionally-minded houses still use oak barrels.

Once fermented, the wines (which may be from different vintages, vineyards, and grapes) are blended together. Before bottling, an additional solution of yeast, sugar, and wine (*liqueur de tirage*) is added, causing a second fermentation in the bottle which produces the bubbles. Sealed with crown caps, the bottles mature on their sides for up to three years, after which they are regularly turned and gradually tilted—or "riddled" (*remuage*)—until vertical, causing the sediment created during the second fermentation to fall into the neck of the bottle. The necks are frozen and the icy pellet of sediment is expelled by removing the cap—the pressure of the fizzy wine forcing the icy

plug out (*dégorgement*). Prior to corking and labeling, a mixture of wine and sugar (*liqueur d'expédition*) is introduced to the bottle (*dosage*).

The resulting sparkling wine is generally dry and white, although sweet champagnes, rosé champagnes, and champagnes made solely from Chardonnay (known as Blanc de Blancs) or from Pinot Noir, sometimes in combination with Pinot Meunier (known as Blanc de Noirs) can also be found. "Extra Brut" is the driest category of sparkling champagne followed by "Brut," both of which, confusingly, are drier even than "Extra Dry" or "Extra Sec"; "Sec" is still less dry, "Demi-Sec" is noticeably sweet, while "Doux" is the sweetest of all.

FINE VINTAGES

1990, 1995, 1996, 1997, 1998, 1999, 2000.

TIP

It is best to serve champagne in "tulips" or "flutes" which retain the wine's effervescence, rather than those shallow "saucers"—allegedly modeled on Marie-Antoinette's breasts—which allow the sparkle to dissipate far too quickly.

MAJOR RED GRAPES

Cabernet Franc, Pinot Noir.

MAJOR WHITE GRAPES

Sauvignon Blanc, Chenin Blanc.

KEY PRODUCERS

André Dezat, de Ladoucette, Alphonse Mellot, Domaine Vacheron, Claude Lafond, Gratien et Meyer, Langlois-Chateau, Henry Pellé, Jacques Rouzé, Olga Raffault.

WINES TO LOOK FOR

Sancerre, Pouilly-Fumé, Muscadet, Vouvray, Savennières, Quincy, Ménétou-Salon, Chinon, Bourgueil, Sauvignon de Touraine, Saumur.

FINE VINTAGES

1990, 1995, 1996, 1997, 1998, 1999, 2000, 2001, 2002, 2003.

TIP

Try a sweet Vouvray as an alternative to Sauternes.

THE LOIRE

The vineyards of the Loire Valley stretch for almost 1,000 miles, producing some truly delightful wines.

Most of the production is devoted to dry white wine, and the area as a whole is a haven for those who subscribe to the ABC (Anything But Chardonnay) fellowship, for this is resolutely Sauvignon Blanc and Chenin Blanc country.

The region is most famous for its Sauvignon Blancs from around the towns of Sancerre and Pouilly-sur-Loire—the dry and zesty Sancerres and Pouilly-Fumés. New Zealanders will surely disagree, but when they're as they should be these are some of the most complex and elegant Sauvignons in the world. Other fine Sauvignons include wines such Ménétou-Salon, Quincy, and Reuilly. These are excellent value alternatives to the bigger names of the region.

Muscadet, less highly regarded but equally well-known, is also made in the Loire, from the Muscadet grape. It is at its best as Muscadet-sur-Lie, meaning that it has been aged on its lees (the sediment left after fermentation), giving it weight and character.

Vouvray is a name to conjure with. Its wines are all made from Chenin Blanc and can come in sparkling, dry, or sweet styles. The botrytis-affected sweet wines are highly sought-after and make a fine alternative to Sauternes and Barsacs.

Chenin Blanc is also used in Saumur to make sparkling wines, which, although vibrant and drinkable, do not have the depth or character of champagne.

There is plenty of rosé found in the region, most particularly the prettily-colored, but unexciting Rosé d'Anjou. Better to stick to the light and delicate Loire reds. Bourgueil and Chinon are the best examples—both made from Cabernet Franc—although the red and rosé Sancerre made from Pinot Noir are a joy to drink, and benefit from an hour or so in the fridge.

FINE VINTAGES

1990, 1992, 1993, 1995,
1996, 1997, 1998, 1999,
2000, 2001, 2002, 2003.

TIP

Try one of the sublimely sweet
and sticky Sélection de Grains
Nobles, not with dessert, but
with a really stinky cheese.

ALSACE

Alsace has some claim to being one of the prettiest of all wine regions.

Tucked away between the Vosges Mountains and the River Rhine in the far northeast of France, it boasts enchanting medieval villages of half-timbered houses, cobbled streets, and tinkling fountains, none of which give any clue to the area's troubled history, which saw Alsace switch this way and that between French and German control thanks to the Franco-Prussian war of 1870 and the First and Second World Wars.

These dizzying changes of nationality can make the wines of Alsace appear somewhat confusing at first sight, coming as they do in the tall green bottles more associated with German wines. The producers and their villages often have German-sounding names, many of which appear on the labels in gothic lettering.

In fact, Alsace is one of the easiest and one of the most rewarding of all of France's wine regions to get to grips with. Most importantly for the winelover new to the region, Alsace has always marketed its wines by grape variety, rather than by the name of the village or the château where the wine was made. Not only that, if it says "Gewurztraminer" on the label, then the wine will be 100 percent Gewurztraminer. This is in contrast to the New World where, say, a Sauvignon Blanc from New Zealand need only be 85 percent Sauvignon and might well contain up to 15 percent Semillon.

There are two ACs for still wines in Alsace—AC Alsace and AC Alsace Grand Cru—with seven main grape varieties being used (see right), the vast majority of which are white. Indeed, Alsace produces about one fifth of all France's still white wines. As well as fragrant, aromatic, spicy-but-dry white wines that are packed with flavor, Alsace's specialty is its sublime Vendanges Tardives, which are late-picked wines of staggering intensity, and the botrytis-affected Sélection de Grains Nobles. Some sparkling wine, called Crémant d'Alsace, is made as well as small amounts of extremely drinkable, but little seen, Pinot Noir.

MAJOR RED GRAPES
Pinot Noir.

MAJOR WHITE GRAPES
Sylvaner, Pinot Blanc, Pinot Gris, Riesling, Gewurztraminer, Muscat.

KEY PRODUCERS
Léon Beyer, Paul Blanck, Dopff Au Moulin, Hugel et Fils, Josmeyer et Fils, Kuentz-Bas, Gustave Lorentz, Mittnacht Frères, Schlumberger, Bruno Sorg, F.E. Trimbach, Zind-Humbrecht, Faller.

WINES TO LOOK FOR
The grapes most closely associated with Alsace are the spicy and pungent Gewurztraminer, the pure and reminiscent of gasoline Riesling and the smoky and creamy Pinot Gris.

THE REST OF FRANCE

Even if you never bought another bottle from France's top regions, you could still be awash with French wine.

About a third of all the country's wines are planted in Languedoc-Roussillon, with the region accounting for almost 80 percent of all France's vins de pays. This massive area runs eastwards from the Spanish border in the southwest to just beyond Montpellier and Nîmes, with the neighboring region of Provence stretching more or less from Marseilles up to the border with Italy. There are some very exciting wines here: the region has been revolutionized by New World winemakers flocking in to weave their magic on the ancient *terroir*, while experimenting with non-indigenous grape varieties. Their influence can also be seen in the way many of these wines are marketed. Much to the irritation of traditionalists and the delight of consumers, the names of the grape varieties used are now appearing on the labels.

In the far southwest, there are big fruity and spicy reds such as Côtes du Roussillon, Fitou, Corbières, and Minervois made from traditional varieties like Carignan, Cinsault, Grenache, Mourvèdre, and Syrah. Cabernet Sauvignon is also beginning to poke its nose in. There is a very fine sparkling wine called Blanquette de Limoux, as well as lip-smacking Vins Doux Naturels such as Muscat de Rivesaltes and the port-like Banyuls. Further to the east there are other reds to be found such as St. Chinian and Faugères.

Provence is home to wines such as Côtes de Provence, Bandol, Palette, and Cassis. Much of the production here is rosé although some fairly anonymous whites are also being made.

Jura and Savoie lie in the east of France, tucked between Burgundy and the Swiss and Italian borders. The specialties of Jura are the quirky dry and sherry-like Vin Jaune, made from Savagnin, and the long-lived Vin de Paille. Some dry whites are made from Savagnin and—increasingly—Chardonnay, alongside some light and fruity reds from Pinot Noir and Poulsard. The wines of Savoie are mainly white, light, and refreshing, made from grapes such as Altesse (also known as Roussette), Jacquère, and Chasselas. There are some pretty decent sparkling wines here, too, as well as a handful of reds made from Mondeuse.

Bergerac is a highly regarded region lying to the east of Bordeaux, which produces claret-like reds and the delicious sweet Monbazillacs which, on a good day, can give the wines of Sauternes a run for their money. Between Bordeaux in the north and the Pyrenees in the south, there are wines such as Cahors—deep, intense reds made from Malbec, Merlot and Tannat—and Madiran—tannic reds also from Tannat. Gaillac makes wines of all hues while the white Jurançon comes sweet or dry. Decent Sauvignon Blanc-based white wines come from Côtes de Duras and reds from Côtes du Frontonnais.

ITALY

VALLE
D'AOSTA

PIEDMONT

LIGURIA

LOMBARDY

Milan

TRENTINO
ALTO
ADIGE FRIULI-
VENEZIA
GIULIA

VENETO Venice

EMILIA-
ROMAGNA

LE MARCHE

Florence

TUSCANY

UMBRIA

ABRUZZO

Rome

LAZIO

PUGLIA

Naples

BASILICATA

SARDINIA

CAMPANIA

Cagliari

CALABRIA

Palermo

SICILY

Italy exports more wine than any other country and the best wine that you have ever drunk may well have come from this wonderful, bewitching, perplexing country. But so might the worst.

NORTHWEST ITALY

Piedmont, whose name means literally "mountain foot," lies at the foot of the Alps and is by far the most important region in Italy's northwest as far as most wine lovers are concerned, although Liguria, Lombardy, and Valle d'Aosta should not be overlooked.

Piedmont (usually called Piemonte in Italian) produces the country's best-known sparkling wine, Asti, as well as what some consider to be Italy's finest red wines, Barolo and Barbaresco, both made from Nebbiolo. Other Nebbiolo-based reds include Gattinara and Ghemme, while Barbera is used to make Barbera d'Asti, Barbera d'Alba, and Barbera del Monferrato, and Dolcetto to make Dolcetto d'Alba and Dolcetto di Dogliani. Barolo is a big, heavy wine full of flavor and, when young, tannin. The best examples need plenty of bottle age after which they soften out, displaying an earthy combination of chocolate and violets. These are wines that last.

Sparkling Asti is made from Moscato grapes and the wines are generally either sweet or semi-sweet, and although much-mocked by connoisseurs, a well-chilled, well-made Asti makes a refreshing and engagingly frivolous aperitif, not least because it is light in alcohol. Gavi is the main white wine of Piedmont. Made from Cortese, it is pleasantly dry and creamy with hints of apple.

Liguria is a little known region tucked between Provence and Tuscany, whose best wine is a fruity and refreshing red called Rossese di Dolceacqua. Lombardy, whose capital is Milan, makes Lugana, a light dry white, and the top class *méthode traditionelle* sparklers from Franciacorta. The French-speaking Valle d'Aosta claims to be Italy's smallest wine growing region and is planted with many varieties, both local and international, few of which seem to be exported.

OPPOSITE, **SCRIMAGLIO WINERY, PIEDMONT**.

MAJOR RED GRAPES
Nebbiolo, Barbera, Dolcetto.

MAJOR WHITE GRAPES
Moscato (Muscat), Pinot Bianco, Trebbiano, Pinot Grigio.

KEY PRODUCERS
Gaja, Giacosa, Fontanafredda, Elio Grasso.

WINES TO LOOK FOR
Barbaresco, Barolo, Spanna, Ghemme, Gattinara, Asti, Moscato d'Asti, Dolcetto d'Alba, sparkling Franciacorta.

FINE VINTAGES
1990, 1991, 1994, 1995, 1996, 1997, 1998, 1999, 2000, 2001.

TIP
The big, hefty reds of the region go especially well with roasts and hearty stews.

MAJOR RED GRAPES

Corvina, Rondinella, Molinara, Cabernet Sauvignon, Merlot, Teroldego, Refosco.

MAJOR WHITE GRAPES

Garganega, Trebbiano, Chardonnay, Malvasia, Pinot Bianco, Pinot Grigio.

KEY PRODUCERS

Masi, Allegrini, Boscaini, Tedeschi, Guerrieri-Rizzardi, Alois Lageder, Collavini, Maculan, Santa Sofia, Schioppetto, Tedeschi.

WINES TO LOOK FOR

Bardolino, Valpolicella, Soave, Prosecco, Bianco di Custoza.

FINE VINTAGES

1990, 1991, 1994, 1995, 1996, 1997, 1998, 1999, 2000, 2001.

TIP

Many wines are made by co-operatives and can be of extremely variable quality. Look at the producer's name and if you find a wine you like, remember it.

NORTHEAST ITALY

The main wine-growing regions of northeast Italy are the Veneto, the Alto Adige, Trentino, and Friuli-Venezia Giulia.

The Veneto is Italy's largest producer of DOC (Denominazione di Origine Controllata) wines. This is where you will find those wine bar standards Valpolicella, Bardolino (both of which are red), and Soave (white). Both the red wines are made from blends of local varieties. Although Soave (made from Trebbiano and Garganega) can be thin and insipid, good ones come from the Classico area and, although hard to find, are deliciously zesty. Look out for the sparkling Prosecco which can be an absolute delight (especially when mixed with fresh peach juice to make a Bellini). Recioto, a wine made from partially dried grapes, is a local specialty, with Recioto di Soave being intensely sweet, and Recioto della Valpolicella, a wine of depth and high alcohol (up to 16 percent), being either sweet or dry (Amarone).

The Alto Adige is also sometimes known as the Sud Tirol and in many ways it is more Austrian than Italian. Part of Austria until 1918, German still remains the main language for most of its inhabitants,

something that is reflected in the Germanic names of the grape varieties and producers. Among the best wines are some light and fragrant Gewurztraminers.

Trentino doesn't have much to recommend among its wines and most of the production is in the hands of large cooperatives. Müller-Thurgau and Chardonnay are the main white grapes, with Cabernet Sauvignon, Merlot, and the local Teroldego being the main red ones.

Friuli-Venezia Giulia has an absurd number of grape varieties at its disposal. It is unlikely that anyone has bothered to count them, but a rough estimate numbers them at 80 or so. The main white variety being Tocai—although Chardonnay, Pinot Grigio, and Pinot Bianco are also grown.

FINE VINTAGES

1990, 1991, 1994, 1995, 1996,
1997, 1998, 1999, 2000, 2001.

TIP

The "Super Tuscans" are among
the finest wines in the world and
repay lengthy aging.

CENTRAL ITALY

Central Italy is divided neatly into six main wine-growing regions— Emilia-Romagna, Tuscany, Le Marche, Umbria, Lazio, and Abruzzo.

Emilia-Romagna produces rather better food than it does wine. Bologna, the region's capital, gave its name to one of the world's most imitated and abused dishes, Spaghetti Bolognese, and the region deserves eternal thanks for its gift to us of proscuitto and Parmigiano Reggiano cheese. Just as well, because it also inflicted on us the horrors of that red, white, or pink sparkler, Lambrusco.

Tuscany is the most significant region in this part of the country and is home to Italy's best-known, although rarely the best, wine— Chianti. Chianti Classico is the finest. The big and beefy Brunello di Montalcino also comes from here, as does Vino Nobile di Montepulciano (Montepulciano in this instance being the town, not the grape).

In the 1970s several producers in Tuscany started to make wines outside the DOC/DOCG regulations, using non-indigenous and unapproved grape varieties, such as Cabernet Sauvignon and Merlot along with the local Sangiovese, and non-traditional methods and techniques. Such was the remarkable quality

and stunning intensity of these wines, they soon came to be known as "Super Tuscans" and even though they were officially ranked at the bottom of the pile as mere table wines, in truth they were among the finest that the region produced. Today, wines such as Sassicaia, Ornellaia, Tignanello, Solaia, Tavernelle, and others rival the best red wines in the world, with many having finally been accorded official status. That curiosity, Vin Santo, much loved by diners who dunk their biscotti in it, also comes from Tuscany.

The best-known wine of Le Marche is the dry white Verdicchio. However, big, juicy Sangiovese/Montepulciano reds such as Rosso Conero and Rosso Piceno are also well worth searching out.

Umbria's wines include Montefalco and Torgiano, although it is Orvieto, named after the medieval hilltop town, that is best known. This can be dry, medium, or sweet, and at its best it is a rich and honeyed wine with a certain nutty character.

Nearly all the wines from Lazio are white, with Frascati being the best known. Who hasn't had a bottle of this in the local wine bar and just about lived to regret it? There are supposedly decent examples of it around, but they are hard to find.

Abruzzo is justly celebrated for its rich and juicy red wine, Montepulciano d'Abruzzo (Montepulciano in this instance being the grape, not the town).

MAJOR RED GRAPES
Sangiovese, Brunello, Canaiolo Nero, Montepulciano, and, increasingly, Cabernet Sauvignon.

MAJOR WHITE GRAPES
Trebbiano, Malvasia, Lambrusco, Vernaccia, Verdicchio, Sauvignon Blanc, Pinot Grigio, Pinot Bianco, Chardonnay.

KEY PRODUCERS
Antinori, Avignonesi, Isole e Olena, Ruffino, Bigi, Fontana Candida, Lungarotti, Le Terrazze, Biondi-Santi, Frescobaldi, Castelli di Ama, Castellare, Villa Pigna.

WINES TO LOOK FOR
Chianti, Brunello di Montalcino, Vino Nobile di Montepulciano, Orvieto, Frascati, Lambrusco, Rosso Piceno, Rosso Conero, Verdicchio, Vernaccia di San Gimignano.

MAJOR RED GRAPES

Aglianico, Barbera, Sangiovese, Gaglioppo, Primitivo, Montepulciano, Gaglioppo.

MAJOR WHITE GRAPES

Greco, Trebbiano, Pinot Bianco.

KEY PRODUCERS

Azienda Nuova Murgia, Leone de Castris, Rivera, d'Angelo, Calatrasi, Corvo, de Bartoli, Donnafugata, Florio, Regaleali, Settesoli, Castel del Monte.

WINES TO LOOK FOR

Marsala, Aglianico del Vulture, Lacryma Christi del Vesuvio, Il Falcone.

FINE VINTAGES

1990, 1991, 1994, 1995, 1996, 1997, 1998, 1999, 2000, 2001.

TIP

The region's wines are ideal for drinking in a trattoria on the quayside in Palermo or watching DVDs of *Cinema Paradiso*.

SOUTHERN ITALY

Apulia (which is generally known to us as Puglia), Basilicata, Calabria, Campania, Sicily, and Sardinia are the main wine producing regions of southern Italy.

A massive amount of wine is made here, but currently the wines are good rather than remarkable. But it is a question of "watch this space," for the climate in southern Italy is ideal and standards are improving all the time. It won't be long before wines of real quality are produced.

Apulia probably makes the finest wines, nearly all of which are red although some rosés and whites can be found, too. A large proportion of the wine produced gets made into vermouth.

Campania's most famous wine, which can be red, white, or rosé, is the bizarrely-named Lacryma Christi del Vesuvio. The main grape of the region is Aglianico, which supposedly has been grown here since 7th century B.C. The reds are big, solid, and tannic, and the whites, such as Greco di Tufo, are dry or sweetly sparkling.

There are more acres under vine in Sicily than anywhere else in Italy, with much of the production going to distillation rather than table wine. The island's greatest contribution to the wine world is its fortified wine, Marsala. Like many fortified wines, this has largely fallen out of favor with wine drinkers, and it is more usually to be found in a kitchen cabinet—as the vital ingredient for zabaglione or veal in Marsala—than it is in the wine cellar. This is a shame as it is a deliciously rich, sherry-like wine that makes an excellent aperitif or digestif.

As with the rest of the region, the wines of Sardinia are getting better, with drinkable reds made from Cannonau, better-known as Grenache. Basilicata's only wine of note is the big, spicy red called Aglianico del Vulture.

In the toe of Italy, Calabria produces red and white wines, the best of which is Cirò—whites from Greco and Trebbiano, and reds and rosés from Gaglioppo.

SPAIN

RIAS BAIXAS

RIBEIRO

VALDEORRAS

TORO

RUEDA

RIBERA DEL DUERO

RIOJA

NAVARRA

SOMONTANO

CARINENA

CALATAYUD

PRIORAT

PENEDÈS

TARRAGONA

Barce

• Madrid

LA MANCHA

UTIEL-REQUENA

• Valencia

VALENCIA

YECLA

VALDEPENAS

JUMILLA

CONDADO DE HUELVA

MONTILLA-MORILES

• Seville

Cádiz

JEREZ & MANZANILLA

Spain has more land under vine than any other country and produces innumerable styles of wine, even though for many of us Spain means only Rioja.

FINE VINTAGES

1991, 1992, 1994, 1995,
1996, 1998, 1999, 2000,
2001, 2002.

TIP

Be adventurous! There
is more to Spain than
just Rioja and there are
some fascinating wines
being made.

CENTRAL NORTH-EAST SPAIN

The wines of Rioja are the most celebrated in Spain, and the best are very fine indeed.

In winemaking terms the Rioja region, which is centred around the town of Logroño in the Ebro Valley, is divided into three: Rioja Alta, Rioja Alavesa and Rioja Baja. Nearly all the production is red, with the main grape grown being Tempranillo. Some wines are made from this unblended, whilst others have additional dollops of Garnacha (the Southern Rhône's Grenache), Graciano and Mazuelo (known as Carignan in Languedoc-Roussillon). Whites are made from Viura (Macabeo), Malvasia Riojana and Garnacha Blanca.

Traditionally, Rioja spends time in oak barrels (a process that leads to those familiar and beguiling whiffs of vanilla) and the label will tell you for how long. Sin Crianza means no time spent in barrel; Crianza will have spent at least six months in barrel and had a total of two years ageing; Reserva is aged for at least three years, with one year in barrel and Gran Reserva will have spent at least two years in oak and three in bottle.

Navarra used to be best-known for its very quaffable rosés, but has recently emerged as a producer of really fine red wines. Its five regions are Valdizarbe, Tierra Estella, Ribera Alta, Baja Montaña and Ribera Baja. The grapes used in Rioja are also grown here along with more familiar varieties such as Cabernet Sauvignon, Merlot and Chardonnay.

Penedès is where most of Spain's sparkling wine, Cava (made from Parellada, Macabeo, Xarel-lo, and sometimes Chardonnay), comes from. At its best, this is a light, refreshing and cheap alternative to champagne, at its worst it is best avoided. There are also some interesting whites made from Chardonnay or Sauvignon Blanc as well as easy-drinking reds from Cabernet Sauvignon, Merlot or Tempranillo.

Other regions to look out for include Priorato, which makes some wonderfully deep and intense reds from international varieties, Costers del Segre, whose reputation is growing rapidly, Tarragona, Somontano, Cariñena, Calatayud and Campo de Borja.

MAJOR RED GRAPES

Tempranillo, Garnacha (Grenache), Mazuelo (Carignan), Graciano

MAJOR WHITE GRAPES

Viura (Macabeo), Malvasia Riojana, Garnacha Blanca, Parellada, Xarel-lo.

KEY PRODUCERS

Rioja: Marqués de Riscal, Marqués de Cáceres, Marqués de Vargas, Marqués de Murrieta, Marqués del Romeral, Marqués del Puerto, Montecillo, Finca Allende, CVNE, Contino, La Rioja Alta, Juan Alcorta. Navarra: Julián Chivite, Ochoa, Guelbenzu. Penedès: Miguel Torres, Parés Baltà, Puig Roca. Cava: Cordoníu, Freixenet. Priorato: Costers del Siurana, Celler Vall-Llach. Costers del Segre: Raïmat, Castel de Remei.

WINES TO LOOK FOR

Red Rioja, Priorato, Navarra.

MAJOR RED GRAPES

Garnacha, Mencía, Tempranillo, Cabernet Sauvignon.

MAJOR WHITE GRAPES

Albariño, Palomino, Torrentés, Godello, Verdejo, Viura.

KEY PRODUCERS

Rías Baixas: Fillaboa, Martin Códax.
Rueda: Castilla la Vieja,
Alvarez y Diez.
Ribera del Duero: Alejandro
Fernández, Aalto, Mariano García,
Vega Sicilia, Emilio Moro.
Toro: Fariña, Viña Bajoz.
Cigales: Valdelosfrailes.
Bierzo: Alvaro Palacios, Dominio
de Tares, Castell de Remei.

WINES TO LOOK FOR

Vega Sicilia, Pingus, Flor de Pingus.

FINE VINTAGES

1990, 1991, 1994, 1995, 1996,
1998, 1999, 2001, 2002, 2003.

TIP

Look out for Albariño whites.

CENTRAL NORTHWEST SPAIN

This coastal and inland region lies in the provinces of Galicia and Castilla y León, north and north-east of Portugal.

The River Duero is the Spanish end of what the Portuguese call the River Douro. Ribera del Duero is home to some of Spain's finest wines, including the country's most famous—Vega Sicilia, a red wine of staggering long-lived power and intensity.

Like Rioja, Tempranillo is the main red grape, although it is often known here as Tinta Fino or Tinta del País, but small amounts of Cabernet Sauvignon are also grown. Wines from here might be becoming expensive, but they are worth seeking out as an excellent alternative to Rioja. In this age of increasing uniformity, with Chardonnay and Cabernet Sauvignon being grown the world over, it is refreshing to find wines made from traditional local varieties.

Cool climate Rías Baixas is best-known for its white wines, most of which are made from unblended Albariño grapes or indigenous and unexciting hybrid varieties.

Toro is currently very fashionable among wine lovers and makes big-boned, high alcohol red wines from Tempranillo (which goes by yet another name here—Tinto de Toro) with an added splash of Garnacha. Ribeiro's whites—made from Godello—are rather better than its reds—made chiefly from Garnacha.

Rueda is a white-wine-growing part of the country, producing aromatic, crisp wines from Verdejo and, occasionally, from Sauvignon Blanc, which usually represent great value.

Bierzo and Cigales are both regions to watch, the former making light and juicy reds from Mencía, the latter making fuller-flavored wines from Tempranillo.

Valdeorras makes decent reds from Mencía blended with Garnacha or Cabernet Sauvignon and crisp whites from Godello and slightly flatter, less exciting ones from Palomino, a grape far better suited to its role in making sherry. Much of the production here is for blending into generic Spanish wine. Other regions that you are less likely to come across wine from include Monterrei and Ribeira Sacra.

CENTRAL & SOUTHERN SPAIN

FINE VINTAGES

There is much less variation between vintages here, and much of the production is blended from different years anyway.

TIP

Although none of the wines quite reach the heights of those made further north, there are plenty of very drinkable examples made in this bottom half of Spain.

There are some fascinating wines being made in these regions, from traditional grape varieties but with improved vinification, and although none have yet reached the heights of Rioja or Ribera del Duero, there is much in these less fashionable parts of Spain to fascinate the enterprising wine lover.

from Airén, Spain's most widely planted grape variety. Further to the east, Utiel-Requena makes easy-drinking reds and rosés from Bobal and Tempranillo, and in the bottom right hand corner of Spain, Alicante makes hefty, dark, alcoholic reds from Monastrell, or, less often, Garnacha Tintorera (a grape that is sometimes called Alicante after its home region and which should not be confused with the other more widespread Garnacha).

Further inland, Yecla, Jumilla, and Bullas make big Monastrell reds and Macabeo whites. Most of Almansa's production is red, mainly from Garnacha Tintorera, Monastrell, and Tempranillo.

In the deep south of Spain, Málaga used to be famous for its raisin-like sweet wines made from Pedro Ximénez and Moscatel, and although some are still made here, production is on the wane. Montilla-Moriles makes an excellent, all too-often overlooked —and invariably cheaper—alternative to sherry from Pedro Ximénez rather than Palomino. And it is worth remembering that good Montilla is better than bad sherry.

Towards the Portuguese border, Condado de Huelva produces fairly ordinary table wine and some sherry-like wines from the local Zalema, similar to, but not nearly as good as, those from the neighboring region of Jerez (see the section on fortified wines) a little further along the coast.

La Mancha, in the center of the country, is the largest demarcated wine region in Europe, producing quantity rather than quality on the whole. There are one or two modern estates producing fine reds from Tempranillo (known here and in some parts of southern Spain as Cencibel), but in general the region churns out simple, but enjoyable and great value easy-drinking wines.

At the foot of La Mancha, Valdepeñas produces flavorful and oaky red wines also from Tempranillo, and plenty of white made

MAJOR RED GRAPES

Garnacha, Monastrell (Mourvèdre), Cencibel (Tempranillo), Cabernet Sauvignon, Merlot, Bobal.

MAJOR WHITE GRAPES

Macabeo, Chardonnay, Airén, Moscatel, Malvasia.

KEY PRODUCERS

La Mancha: Dehesa del Carrizal, Dominio de Valdepusa, Félix Solís, Finca Élez, Alejandro Fernandéz, Castillo de Alhambra.

Valdepeñas: J A Megía & Hijos, Los Llanos, Luís Megía, Casa de la Viña.

Alicante: Gutíerrez de la Vega.

Montilla-Moriles: Alvear, Perez Barquero, Gracia Hermanos.

Almansa: Piqueras.

Valencia: Agapito Rico.

WINES TO LOOK FOR

The sherry-like wines of Montilla.

PORTUGAL

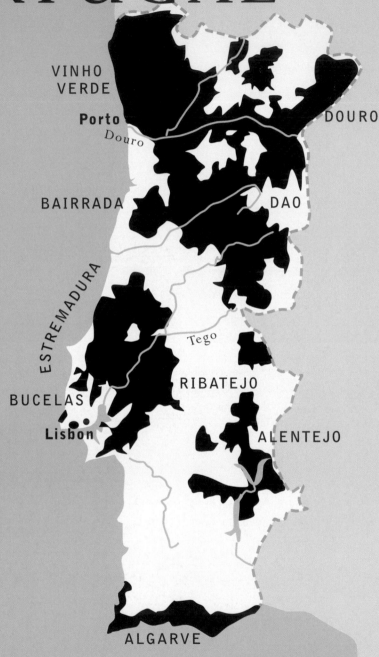

VINHO
VERDE

Porto

Douro

DOURO

BAIRRADA

DAO

ESTREMADURA

Tego

BUCELAS

RIBATEJO

Lisbon

ALENTEJO

ALGARVE

Inevitably, Portugal is best known for its fortified wine, port, and, sadly, for its Mateus Rosé, but there is much more to this country than either of these, with some delicious new-wave table wines now being made.

PORTUGAL

MAJOR RED GRAPES

Touriga Nacional, Tinta Roriz/Aragonez (Tempranillo), Tinta Borroca, Trincadeira, Touriga Franca, Tinta Cão, Baga.

MAJOR WHITE GRAPES

Alvarinho, Azal Branco, Loureiro, Trajadura, Arinto.

KEY PRODUCERS

Quinta de la Rosa, Niepoort, Quinta do Vale Dona Maria, Prats and Symington, Quinta do Roriz, Quinta do Soval, Sogrape, Luís Pato, Quinta do Crasto, Quinta do Vale Meão, Real Campanhia Velha, Quinta da Aveleda, Quinta do Carmo.

WINES TO LOOK FOR

Barca Velha, Vinho Verde, Chryseia, Bairrada, Dão, Douro, Setúbal, Bucellas Velho, Perequita.

FINE VINTAGES

1995, 1998, 2000, 2001, 2002, 2003.

TIP

Portugal has more to offer the wine lover than just port. There are some fine, powerful reds beginning to be made and they can only get better.

The vast majority of Portuguese wines continue to be made from quirky local grape varieties that you simply won't see anywhere else. Many are still sold in bottles with obscure, hard to follow labels, but things are changing fast.

Portugal is great if you are the adventurous type, searching for new taste sensations and prepared to take pot luck, but not so good if you are wedded to your Chardonnays and Cabernet Sauvignons. But the country has embraced change with gusto, and the old-style, rustic wines aimed firmly at domestic consumption (which is huge, the Portuguese are a thirsty lot) are beginning to give way to ripe and fruity wines, still from their own favorite grape varieties, tailored especially for export.

In northern Portugal, the Douro is port country. As this fortified wine begins to feel the pinch, many of the port houses are putting their considerable weight into making serious table wines, too. Some exciting full-bodied ripe and fruity reds are

now being made. The same goes for Dão—home to hearty, long-lived red wines made chiefly from Tinta Roriz (Portugal's name for Spain's Tempranillo) and Touriga Nacional (the main grape used to make port). In Bairrada, the reds are big, tannic wines made from Baga, a grape you certainly won't see anywhere else.

Vinho Verde (made in the Minho region) is the country's largest DOC area and its production accounts for about a third of

SYMINGTON FAMILY ESTATES.

Portugal's domestic market. When on it's as it should be (and when made from Alvarinho), this is an easy-drinking, light, slightly *pétillant*, refreshing white wine, low in alcohol. When not, it is grimly sharp and acidic. There are red Vinho Verdes, too.

In southern and central Portugal, there are plentiful but ordinary wines made in Estremadura, fruity and easy-drinking reds (including some from Cabernet Sauvignon, Merlot, and Syrah) in Ribatejo, and decent full-flavored whites in Bucelas. Further south there are some interesting new wines being made in the country's largest province, Alentejo, and right at Portugal's tip, even the Algarve is beginning to produce some decent reds.

A curiosity to look out for is Moscatel de Setúbal, an attractive and highly scented fortified wine not dissimilar to Muscat de Beaumes-de-Venise.

Although Germany is despised by many wine lovers for being the mass producer of the dreaded Liebfraumilch, to others it is hugely admired as the source of the finest and purest Rieslings in the world.

MAJOR RED GRAPES

Pinot Noir (a.k.a. Spätburgunder), Dornfelder.

MAJOR WHITE GRAPES

Riesling, Müller-Thurgau, Pinot Blanc (a.k.a. Weissburgunder), Silvaner.

KEY PRODUCERS

Max Ferd Richter, JJ Prüm, Ernst Loosen, Willi Schaefer, Schloss Johnnisberg, Heinrich Seebrich, Carl Sittman, Adolf Lotzbeyer, Koehler-Ruprecht, JB Becker, Josef Leitz, Wolf Metternich, Graf Adelmann, JJ Christoffel, Fritz Haag, Maximin Grünhaus, Schneider, Egon Müller-Scharzhof.

WINES TO LOOK FOR

Although Müller-Thurgau is widely planted, Germany's finest wines are overwhelmingly Rieslings.

FINE VINTAGES

1990, 1992, 1994, 1995, 1997, 1999, 2001, 2002, 2003.

TIP

Some of Germany's most sought-after wines are the late-picked Beerenausleses and Trockenbeerenausleses, which have a fragrance and elegance that are rarely matched by other dessert wines.

GERMANY

Germany really is all about Riesling which, when it is on top of its game, has a major claim to being the finest of all the white grape varieties.

It produces wines of unparalleled purity and elegance, and for those who imagine that German wines are only ever medium-dry, think again, for they can range from the dry Kabinetts to the intensely sweet and honeyed Trockenbeerenauslese and Eiswein.

There are two main wine producing areas in Germany, the Mosel and the Rhine. The region of Mosel-Saar-Ruwer is so-named because of the three rivers which thread the area, the Rivers Saar and Ruwer being tributaries of the Mosel. Only white wines are made here, produced from Riesling, Müller-Thurgau, or Pinot Blanc (known as Weissburgunder). The best-known wine-making towns and villages in the area are Wiltingen and Scharzhofberg in the Saar-Ruwer district and Bernkastel, Piesport, Wehlen, Brauneberg, Graach, Zeltingen, and Erden in the Mittelmosel. Their wines are fragrant and light-bodied with a wonderful steely and racy acidity, the finest wines coming from the steep hillside vineyards which seem to tumble down to the riverside. Wines from the Mosel are historically sold in green bottles, as opposed to the brown bottles of the Rhine, but this is changing.

Liebfraumilch (sigh) comes from the Rhine, but so do some remarkably stylish Rieslings and other white wines, along with light and fruity reds made from Spätburgunder, otherwise known as Pinot Noir. The six wine growing regions of the Rhine are the Ahr, Mittelrhein, Rheingau, Nahe, Rheinhessen, and Pfalz formerly known as Rheinpfalz. Rheinhessen is the largest wine growing region in Germany and includes such villages as Nierstein and Oppenheim. Although dying out, "Hock" (from the village Hockheim) has long been the term given to wines from the Rhine.

Franken produces decent whites, drier than many in Germany, which, far from coming in the tall fluted bottles used in the country's other regions, come in a squat, green flagon, the style for which was allegedly modeled on the scrotum of the goat (and why not?) called a *bocksbeutal*.

Baden also produces dry whites while Württemberg is best-known for making light and fruity Spätburgunder reds. Other regions whose wine you might come across include Hessische Bergstrasse, Sachsen, and Saale-Unstrut.

NORTH AMERICA

The main wine-growing areas in the United States are California, Washington State, and Oregon, although, remarkably enough, wine is now produced in every state in the Union. Canada, too, produces some serious wine.

CALIFORNIA

California is a wine-lover's paradise with a great climate, plenty of investment, some remarkably stylish wineries, and no shortage of genuine "can-do" spirit, leading to some great wines being made.

Although it is true that wines of any quality here have tended to be expensive (and those from the small, chic boutique wineries still are), prices have fallen dramatically over the last couple of years and now it isn't just jug wine that is affordable.

In terms of the export market, California (which is currently the fourth largest producer of wine in the world) is now beginning to compete abroad with the everyday branded wines of Australia, although it is the mid-range wines that are the most interesting and the best value.

The main wine growing regions in California are Mendocino, Sonoma, Napa Valley, and the San Francisco Bay area in the northern part of the state, and Monterey, the Sierra foothills, San Luis Obispo, and Santa Barbara County in the central part of the state.

Zinfandel is celebrated as California's "own grape" and is responsible both for fairly dire off-dry rosés (either called White Zinfandel or Blush Zinfandel) and for wonderful, heady, rich, spicy, jammy reds. But despite the Californians' pride in Zinfandel, the state is really in thrall to Cabernet Sauvignon, which accounts for about a quarter of all red varieties grown there. It thrives especially in the Napa Valley where it produces wines of remarkable depth and intensity. Merlot is popular, too, and so, increasingly, are Syrah, Petite Sirah (very much on the up) and Pinot Noir, which is currently much in vogue thanks to the release in 2005 of the Oscar-winning wine-tasting road movie *Sideways*, which eulogizes the grape. Sales (and plantings) have rocketed, with the variety doing especially well in the cool-climate areas such as Sonoma, Santa Ynez Valley, and Russian River Valley.

MAJOR RED GRAPES

Cabernet Sauvignon, Merlot, Pinot Noir, Zinfandel, Syrah, Petite Sirah.

MAJOR WHITE GRAPES

Chardonnay, Sauvignon Blanc.

KEY PRODUCERS

Chateau Montelena, Clos du Val, Opus One, Bonny Doon, Duckhorn, Mondavi, Joseph Phelps, Saintsbury, Stag's Leap, Clos du Bois, Heitz, Andrew Quady, Screaming Eagle, Au Bon Climat, Freemark Abbey, Far Niente, Marcassin, Frog's Leap, Dominus, Kenwood, Ravenswood, Wente Vineyards, Justin Vineyards, Byron, Schramsberg, Turley Vineyards.

WINES TO LOOK FOR

The best single varietals such as Cabernet Sauvignon and Chardonnay.

It won't be cheap, but try and trade up and treat yourself. A top class, highly concentrated, Cabernet Sauvignon from the Napa Valley really is hard to beat.

Chardonnay is still far and away the most popular white variety in the state—both amongst growers and consumers—and the best are an absolute joy, although there is still a tendency to overwhelm the grape's natural elegance with too much oak.

Sauvignon Blanc is a distant second in terms of white grape popularity, followed by such currently fashionable varieties as Viognier and Roussanne. There are also some spectacular sweet wines and some great value champagne method sparklers to be found.

Despite the continued popularity of the classic varieties, one of the most interesting new developments in the region is the emergence of the so-called Cal-Italian wines, made from such red grapes as Barbera, Dolcetto, Nebbiolo, and Sangiovese and such white grapes as Pinot Grigio. Many of these varieties were brought over by Italian immigrants during the Gold Rush, but it is only recently that winemakers have started to make top class wines from them.

California has an exciting future ahead of it. Thanks to the awful specter of phylloxera, which caused a great devastation in the vineyards in the 1980s and 1990s, there has been extensive replanting throughout the state. This has allowed growers and producers to rethink their strategies and to include better varieties and clones than perhaps they were using before. This is not dissimilar to what occurred in Bordeaux in the 1880s when phylloxera wrought havoc there. The new vines are just coming into fruition and can only get better as they mature.

ABOVE **JORDAN VINEYARD AND WINERY, SONOMA COUNTY** OPPOSITE, ABOVE **DUCKHORN WINERY, NAPA VALLEY** OPPOSITE, BELOW **CANEROS, NAPA VALLEY**.

MAJOR RED GRAPES

Pinot Noir, Merlot.

MAJOR WHITE GRAPES

Pinot Gris, Chardonnay,
Riesling.

**WINES TO LOOK FOR
IN OREGON**

Some really classy Pinot Noirs
to rival those of Burgundy and
New Zealand.

MAJOR RED GRAPES

Merlot, Cabernet Sauvignon,
Syrah.

MAJOR WHITE GRAPES

Chardonnay.

**WINES TO LOOK FOR
IN WASHINGTON STATE**

Bordeaux-style red blends.

MAJOR RED GRAPES

Merlot, Pinot Noir, Cabernet
Franc.

MAJOR WHITE GRAPES

Chardonnay, Riesling,
Gewurztraminer.

**WINES TO LOOK FOR
IN NEW YORK STATE**

Take your pick, and see how
wines from New York improve
with each vintage.

THE PACIFIC NORTHWEST

OREGON

Willamette Valley, west of the Cascade Mountains, is Oregon's main wine growing area
and its cool climate is ideal not only for Pinot Noir but also for white grapes such as Pinot
Gris and Riesling and, to a lesser extent, Sauvignon Blanc, Gewurztraminer, Chardonnay,
and Pinot Blanc.

Oregon's subtle wines are the perfect antidote for those wine lovers who might find the wines
of California and other hot climate areas too ripe, fruit-forward, and full-bodied. People talk
about the region's complex and classy Pinot Noir in tones of hushed awe, as being the wine
that showed the world that this capricious grape could be grown outside of France. Indeed,
for a while in the 1960s, during the early days of the Oregon wine industry, it was the only
grape grown in the state.

WASHINGTON STATE

Most of Washington's wine is grown in the American Viticultural Areas (AVAs) of Columbia
Valley, Yakima Valley, Walla Walla, and Red Mountain. Cabernet Sauvignon is the main red
grape, although Syrah is beginning to find favor. Whites are not always so successful,
although there is some Semillon, Riesling, Chardonnay, and Sauvignon Blanc grown.

NEW YORK STATE

There are some really decent European-style wines being made here in getting-on-for
200 wineries, and the region now makes more wine than Oregon. The main wine making
areas are Lake Erie, Hudson River Valley, Long Island (North Fork and The Hamptons)
and Finger Lakes—the largest.

For too long the region relied on French-American hybrids and local varieties, as well as on
mass-producing grape juice, but, just like neighboring Ontario, the classic varieties are now
being grown with notable success and some fascinating wines are being made. Riesling,
Gewurztraminer and Chardonnay make the best whites, while Cabernet Franc, Pinot Noir, and
Merlot make the best reds.

That vinous curiosity made from frozen grapes, Icewine, which New York shares with Canada,
has become something of a specialty of the region, too. At the moment, very little of New
York State's wines is exported, but this will surely change as the wines continue to improve.

CANADA

It surprises many Europeans that Canada makes wine at all, let alone wine of the very high quality that it does. The wine regions are Niagara Peninsula, Lake Erie North Shore, Pelee Island in Ontario, and Okanagan Valley and Vancouver Island in British Columbia. The grapes that do best are those such as Chardonnay, Riesling, Pinot Gris, and Sauvignon Blanc for whites and Pinot Noir, Cabernet Franc, and Merlot for reds. Cabernet Sauvignon struggles to ripen here.

Canada's gift to the wine world is their Icewine, a remarkably rich and intensely sweet wine made from grapes such as Riesling, Cabernet Franc, and the hybrid variety, Vidal, that have been frozen on the vine—thus concentrating the sugars. It has to be tasted to be believed.

MAJOR RED GRAPES

Merlot, Gamay, Pinot Noir, Syrah.

MAJOR WHITE GRAPES

Pinot Gris, Pinot Blanc, Riesling.

WINES TO LOOK FOR IN CANADA

The astonishing, intensely sweet Icewines.

SOUTH AMERICA

CHILE

ACONCAGUA VALLEY
CASABLANCA VALLEY

Santiago

RAPEL VALLEY
MAULE VALLEY
SAN ANTONIO VALLEY
CENTRAL VALLEY

SALTA

LA RIOJA
SAN JUAN

MENDOZA

• Buenos Aires

RIO NEGRO

ARGENTINA

There are some wonderful wines coming out of South America at the moment. Chile has the edge in terms of quality, but Argentina isn't far behind. Massive investment in both countries promises exciting times ahead.

CHILE

Chile is blessed with ideal conditions for growing grapes, and with recent improvements in winemaking techniques and consistently competitive pricing, it is little wonder that its wines are so popular.

ABOVE, RIGHT, FAR RIGHT ABOVE, & BELOW **ERRAZURIZ DON MAXIMIANO ESTATE, ACONCAGUA VALLEY**.

Along with New Zealand, Chile has been one of the wine world's greatest success stories, with some of Europe's finest producers now clamoring to invest money and expertise in the country.

Chile's wines represent extraordinary value with rich, ripe reds and grassy herbaceous whites at extremely affordable prices. What they might lack in complexity, they more than make up for in good, rich fruit and drinkability. In the past few years the country has also begun to produce some really high-class wines, to rival California's top single vineyards, Italy's "Super Tuscans" and Bordeaux's First Growths. And these wines lack nothing in complexity —if you can afford them.

RIGHT & FAR RIGHT, BELOW & BOTTOM
CONCHA Y TORO, MAIPO VALLEY.

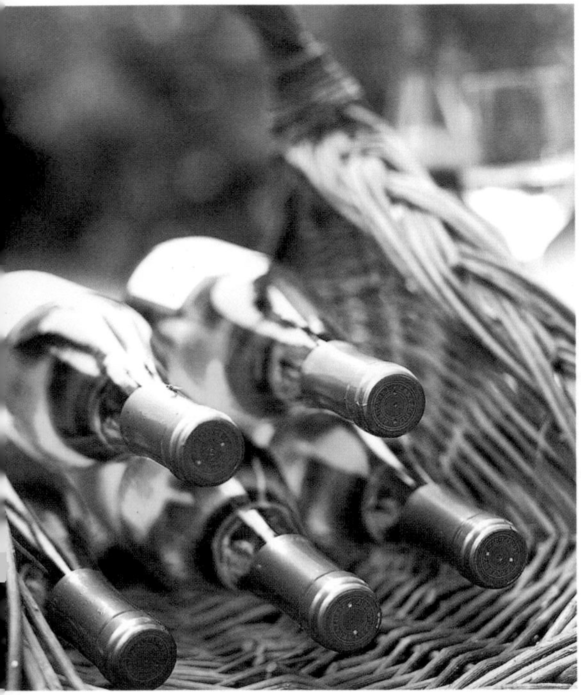

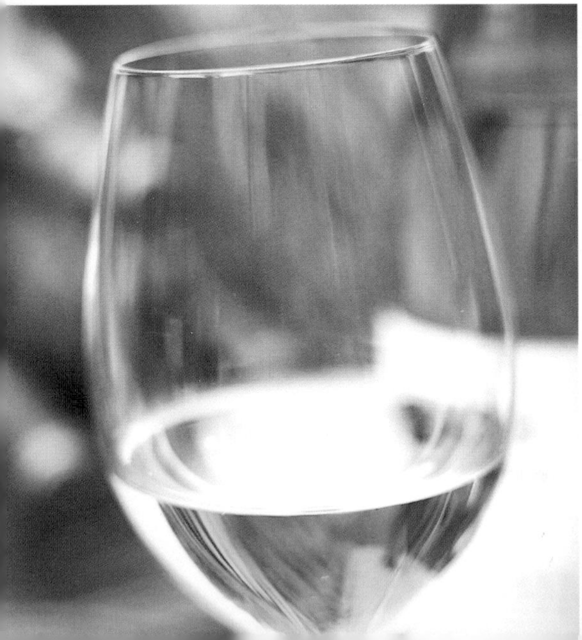

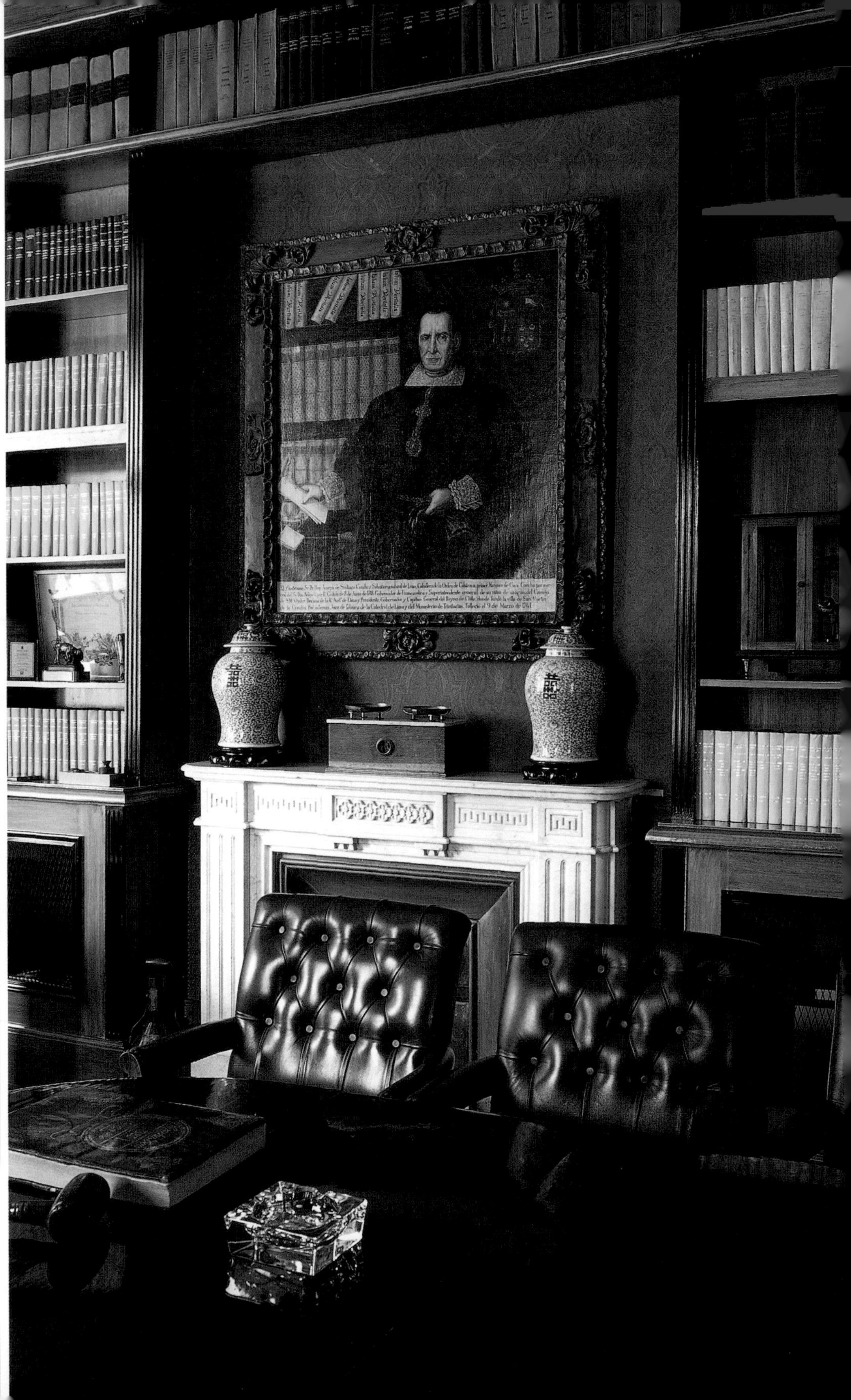

The country's first wines were produced in the 16th century by the Spanish conquerors, largely for communion or home consumption, with the white Mission and red Pais grapes being the most widely planted. During the 1850s, when all things French were in vogue in Chile, well-to-do Chileans began to travel to France, often returning home with cuttings from the vineyards. Since they traveled chiefly to Bordeaux (the most fashionable region at the time) rather than to Burgundy or the Rhône, the varieties that they brought back were predominantly the classic Bordeaux ones —Cabernet Sauvignon, Merlot, Cabernet Franc, and Malbec. As a result, even today, Chile's wines remain closest in style to Bordeaux.

The Central Valley is divided into four smaller regions: The Maipo Valley, south of Santiago, which is particularly well-suited to growing Cabernet Sauvignon and Chardonnay; the Rapel Valley (including the Colchagua Valley) growing Merlot and Cabernet Sauvignon, with increasing plantings of Syrah and Carmenère; the Curicó Valley growing mainly Cabernet Sauvignon with some Merlot and Sauvignon Blanc; and the Maule Valley where red wine production also predominates.

The Aconcagua Valley produces excellent Cabernet Sauvignons, while the cool Casablanca Valley, tucked between Santiago and the Pacific Ocean, is the country's best region for Chardonnay and Sauvignon Blanc. There is some interesting Pinot Noir being grown in the San Antonio Valley.

MAJOR RED GRAPES

Cabernet Sauvignon, Merlot, Syrah, Pinot Noir, Carmenère, Malbec.

MAJOR WHITE GRAPES

Sauvignon Blanc, Chardonnay, Gewurztraminer, Viognier.

KEY PRODUCERS

Errázuriz, Viñedo Chadwick, Caliterra, Cousino-Macul, Miguel Torres, Santa Rita, Montes, Carmen, Casa Lapostolle, Concha y Toro, Cono Sur, Valdivieso, Veramonte, Casa Marin, Almaviva, Casa Marin.

WINES TO LOOK FOR

Viñedo Chadwick, Seña, Almaviva, Clos Apalta, Cuvée Alexandre Merlot.

FINE VINTAGES

1997, 1998, 1999, 2000, 2001, 2003.

TIP

Chile does extremely well in the mid-range price bracket, so look out for Sauvignon Blancs that are grassy and herbaceous, and Merlots and Cabernet Sauvignons which are ripe, fruity, and plummy.

MAJOR RED GRAPES

Malbec, Cabernet Sauvignon, Sangiovese, Syrah, Merlot, Tempranillo, Pinot Noir, Bonarda, Nebbiolo, Tannat.

MAJOR WHITE GRAPES

Chardonnay, Pinot Gris, Sauvignon Blanc, Chenin Blanc, Semillon, Viognier, Torrontés, Salentin.

KEY PRODUCERS

J & F Lurton, Clos de Los Siete, Norton, Catena Zapata, Finca Flichman, Weinert, Humberto Canale, Altos Los Hormigas, Trapiche, San Telmo, Chandon, Familia Zuccardi, Benegas, Cheval des Andes.

WINES TO LOOK FOR

Supple reds made from Malbec.

FINE VINTAGES

1997, 1999, 2000, 2001, 2002, 2003.

TIP

Argentina is particularly good for big, beefy red wines.

ARGENTINA

Argentina is now the fifth largest producer of wine in the world. And even though it has twice as many vineyards as its neighbor, Chile, it has long been perceived as the poor man's equivalent by wine lovers.

But the climate and conditions enjoyed by both countries, and the wines they produce, are very different and so comparisons, although inevitable, are unfair. Chile, with its vineyards near the coast, is influenced by the sea, whereas Argentina, with vineyards some thousand miles inland, is influenced by mountains and desert and, in Mendoza, blistering heat.

Argentina's wines have improved considerably over the last few years, thanks to massive foreign investment, with their reds showing particularly well. Historically, Argentina looked to Italy for its grape varieties whereas Chile looked to Bordeaux, but these distinctions are fading and similar varieties are beginning to be grown. The mostly widely planted red grape in Argentina is Bonarda, but its most important, at least

in terms of export and quality of wine, is Malbec. Here the grape reaches heights that it fails to reach anywhere else, except perhaps Cahors in France, making deep, rich and flavorful wines. It was once a stalwart of the Bordeaux blend, but has long fallen out of favor there.

The main regions are Mendoza (in which about three quarters of the country's vineyards lie), Rio Negro, Salta, San Juan, and La Rioja (not to be confused with the region of the same name in Spain), and the grapes they grow are remarkably diverse.

Mendoza is divided into North Mendoza (best for light, easy-drinking reds made from Sangiovese and Bonarda, and Chenin Blanc whites), Upper Mendoza River (quality Malbec and Cabernet Sauvignon country), Uco Valley (top quality reds and whites from a wide range of varieties), East Mendoza (the province's largest area, producing big, dense reds and full-bodied whites), and South Mendoza (full-flavored Syrahs, Malbecs, and Cabernets, and some Chenin Blancs).

Salta is ideal for vine-growing but is somewhat remote, and mainly makes light Torrontés whites although some decent reds can be found. La Rioja and Rio Negro make both reds and whites, while San Juan is best-known for its fortified wines.

AUSTRALIA

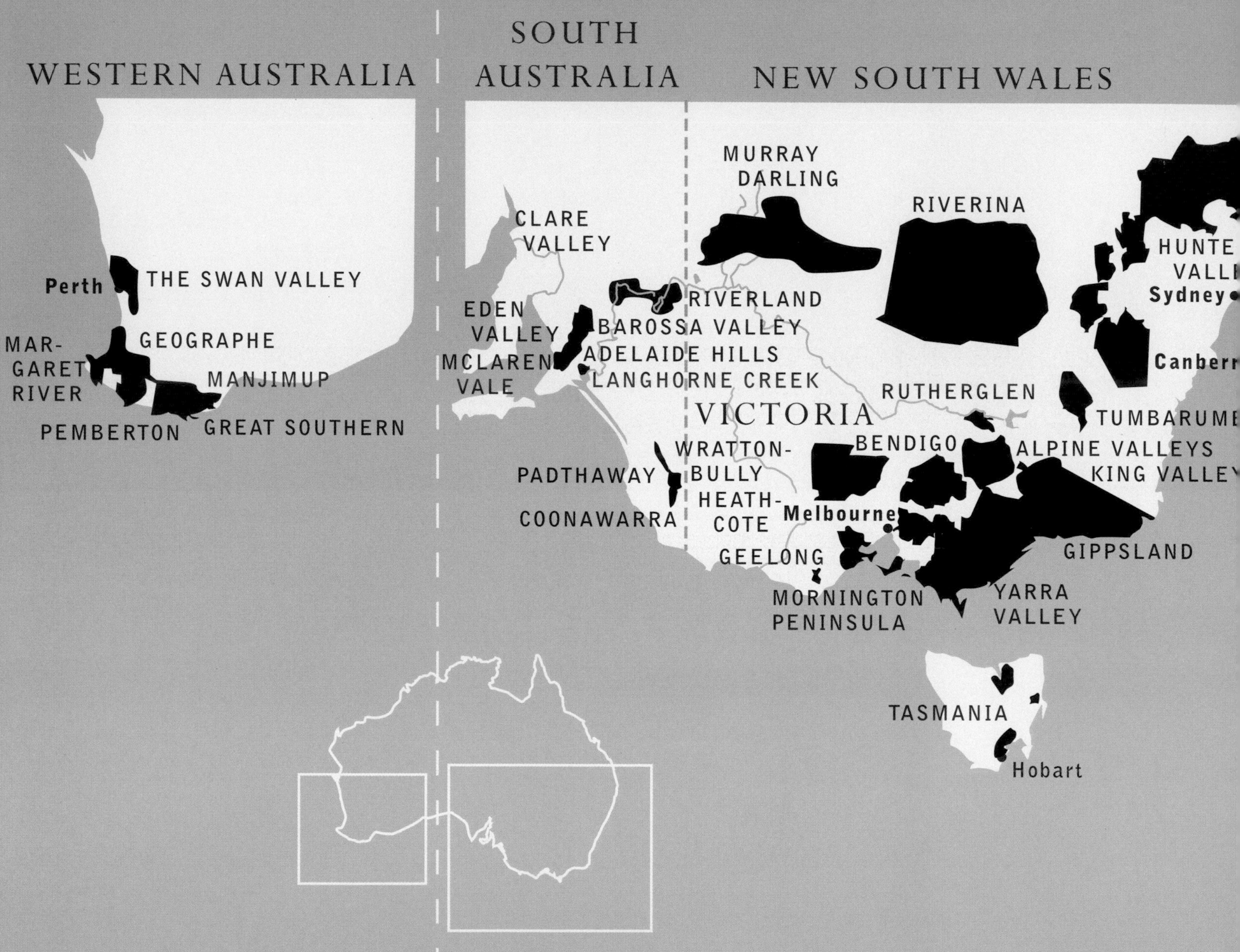

WESTERN AUSTRALIA

SOUTH AUSTRALIA

NEW SOUTH WALES

Perth THE SWAN VALLEY

MAR-
GARET GEOGRAPHE
RIVER
MANJIMUP

PEMBERTON GREAT SOUTHERN

CLARE
VALLEY

EDEN
VALLEY
MCLAREN
VALE

BAROSSA VALLEY

RIVERLAND

ADELAIDE HILLS

LANGHORNE CREEK

MURRAY
DARLING

RIVERINA

HUNTE
VALL
Sydney

Canberr

PADTHAWAY

COONAWARRA

WRATTON-
BULLY

HEATH-
COTE

GEELONG

MORNINGTON
PENINSULA

VICTORIA

Melbourne

BENDIGO

RUTHERGLEN

ALPINE VALLEYS

TUMBARUME

KING VALLEY

YARRA
VALLEY

GIPPSLAND

TASMANIA

Hobart

Australia is the sixth largest wine producer in the world, and now sells more wine than France does in many of its markets. With up-front fruity wines and easy-to-understand labels, Australia has more or less cornered the market for affordable wines, while continuing to produce wines of remarkable quality at the top end.

There is something for everyone in Australia and one could drink nothing but Australian wine for the rest of one's life and die happy.

There are big, powerful, full-bodied Shirazes and Cabernet Sauvignons, oaky Chardonnays and Semillons, elegant Rieslings, and remarkable sweet and fortified wines. And although one could be forgiven for thinking that Australia only produces inexpensive branded wines, there are any number of boutique wineries producing exquisite bottles at much higher prices.

NEW SOUTH WALES

The Hunter Valley, which is divided into the Upper Hunter and the Lower Hunter, is probably Australia's best-known wine region. It is hot here and the wines are big and full-flavored and although a variety of grapes are grown, it is the region's Semillons, Chardonnays, and Shirazes that are most celebrated. The areas of Mudgee, Orange, and Cowra are somewhat in the Hunter Valley's shadow and much cooler, making some fine Chardonnays, Merlots, and Cabernets that are more European in style. Other winemaking regions of note in New South Wales include Hilltops, Canberra District, Riverina, and Tumbarumba.

VICTORIA

There is a strong Italian influence in Victoria, with immigrants having come here to grow tobacco and hops. Following the decline of the cigarette industry, however, many of these families moved on to growing grapes and making wine. And now, thanks to an unusual diversity in soil and climate, Victoria probably grows a greater number of different grape varieties than any other region in the world. A generation ago, about 70 percent of Victoria's wine production was fortified, but now every conceivable style of wine is produced, from dry to sweet, still to sparkling.

Winemaking districts include North East, Central, and South Yarra Valley, Rutherglen, Alpine Valleys, King Valley, Geelong, Gippsland, Bendigo, Mornington Peninsula, and Heathcote.

MAJOR RED GRAPES

Shiraz (a.k.a. Syrah), Cabernet Sauvignon, Merlot, Pinot Noir.

MAJOR WHITE GRAPES

Chardonnay, Semillon, Sauvignon Blanc, Viognier, Riesling, Muscat.

WINES TO LOOK FOR

Henschke's Hill of Grace and Penfolds Grange are iconic wines that are the equal of any in the world.

FINE VINTAGES

Vintages in Australia are relatively consistent, with far less variation than in Europe.

TIP

If you are an ABC ("Anything But Chardonnay") type, it could be because you have fallen foul of an over-oaked Australian cheapie. Don't be put off, because there are some real beauties to be found and you are in danger of missing out on a potential favorite.

SOUTH AUSTRALIA

South Australia is the country's largest wine-producing region and includes such districts as Barossa Valley, Coonawarra, Eden Valley, Adelaide Hills, Clare Valley, McLaren Vale, Langhorne Creek, Kingston, Riverland, Wrattonbully, and Padthaway. The Barossa Valley, north of Adelaide, is hot and dry and produces massive, blockbusting Shirazes as well as fresh and fragrant Rieslings. This is the main source for Australia's finest wine, Penfolds Grange. The Clare Valley is home to some fine Rieslings as well as silky smooth Semillons, while the Eden Valley (home to Henschke's Hill of Grace) produces top quality Rieslings and Shirazes. Clare Valley Rieslings tend to be slightly more austere and less aromatic than those from the Eden Valley.

Coonawarra is Cabernet Sauvignon country, producing wonderful complex and minty reds, while McLaren Vale makes both Cabernet and Shiraz. Top Chardonnays, Sauvignon Blancs, and Pinot Noirs can be found in the cooler Adelaide Hills.

WESTERN AUSTRALIA

Western Australia is an area of quality rather than quantity. The foremost region is Margaret River, about a three hour drive south of Perth. It was first planted with serious vines in the late 1960s and became an overnight success. Today it produces Bordeaux-style reds and wonderful Chardonnays and Sauvignon Blancs. The Swan Valley is bakingly hot and ideal for making fortified wines as well as whites from Chardonnay, Chenin Blanc, and Verdelho.

Other regions include Pemberton, good for Pinot Noir and Chardonnay, Manjimup, Geographe, and Great Southern.

TASMANIA

Tasmania is often overlooked as one of Australia's wine regions, and it is indeed the country's smallest. It wasn't until the late 1970s that it began to be taken seriously, as winemakers struggled to overcome the spring frosts and savage off-sea winds. The four main grapes grown on the island are Chardonnay, Riesling, Sauvignon Blanc, and Pinot Noir, all of which seem to enjoy the cool climate here, although under-ripe grapes can be a problem. Some pretty good sparkling wines are being made, which promise to get even better.

NEW ZEALAND

NORTHLAND

AUCKLAND **Auckland**

WAIHEKE ISLAND BAY OF PLENTY

WAIKATO GISBORNE

NORTH ISLAND HAWKES BAY

WELLINGTON WAIRARAPA

Wellington Martinborough

Nelson MARLBOROUGH

NELSON

WAIPARA

Christchurch

SOUTH ISLAND CANTERBURY

CENTRAL OTAGO

Dunedin

New Zealand is one of the most exciting of all wine producing countries. It has only been producing Sauvignon Blanc for 30 years and some would argue that these wines are now the best of their type in the world. Pinot Noir promises to be just as successful.

NEW ZEALAND

MAJOR RED GRAPES

Cabernet Sauvignon, Merlot, Pinot Noir, Syrah.

MAJOR WHITE GRAPES

Sauvignon Blanc, Chardonnay, Riesling.

KEY PRODUCERS

Cloudy Bay, Sileni Estate, Seresin, Matua Valley, Montana, Craggy Range, Clearview Estate, Te Mata Estate, Te Awa Farm, Alana Estate, Villa Maria, Kumeu River, Palliser Estate, Felton Road, Nga Waka, Fromm.

WINES TO LOOK FOR

The Sauvignon Blancs of Marlborough are among the finest in the world.

FINE VINTAGES

1994, 1996, 1998, 1999, 2000, 2001, 2003.

TIP

Look for the Pinot Noirs of Martinborough and the Bordeaux blends and Syrahs of Hawkes Bay.

New Zealand is one of the great recent success stories of the winemaking world.

Grapes have been grown here since the 1820s, planted originally by European missionaries. Additional varieties were brought by German settlers and the Dalmatian Yugoslavs, who came to dig for kauri gum in North Island. They planted vines around Auckland, the early wines of which became known as "Dally Diesel." It wasn't until the 1960s, though, that producers started to experiment in earnest, with Müller-Thurgau initially deemed to be the most suitable grape for New Zealand. This was widely planted, and produced gallons of well-made but intensely dull imitations of Liebfraumilch.

Then, barely 30 years ago, some bright sparks—namely the Spence brothers at Matua Valley near Auckland—planted some experimental vines of Sauvignon Blanc and, bingo, they hit the jackpot, with Kiwi Sauvignons today regarded as the benchmark to which the world's other winemakers aspire. It was soon discovered that Marlborough was a better region for the grape than Auckland, and today this is where 85 percent of New Zealand's Sauvignon Blanc is grown. Although those raised on the subtle and restrained Sauvignons of the

Loire, such as Sancerre and Pouilly-Fumé, might find these zesty and exuberant wines a bit too much with their grassy, gooseberry, and asparagus flavors (complete with whiff of cat's pee), these wines are world class.

The country's main wine regions are Hawkes Bay (and its sub-region, Gimblett Gravels), Gisbourne, Martinborough (sometimes known as Wairarapa), Waiheke Island, and Matakana in North Island, and Marlborough, Nelson, Waipara, and Central Otago in South Island.

The remarkable success of Sauvignon in New Zealand often obscures the fact that excellent Chardonnays are also made throughout the country, with Pinot Gris and Riesling (the latter chiefly in South Island) not far behind.

The country's finest reds are the Bordeaux-style blends of Hawkes Bay or the Pinot Noirs of Martinborough and Central Otago. The plantings of Pinot Noir in New Zealand have doubled in the last four years, and the grape is now their most widely grown red variety, covering over 8,500 acres. The best are stunning, lip-smacking, and juicy, and if they continue to wiggle their hips in this way, it won't be long before they woo us away from red burgundy or other New World Pinot.

SOUTH AFRICA

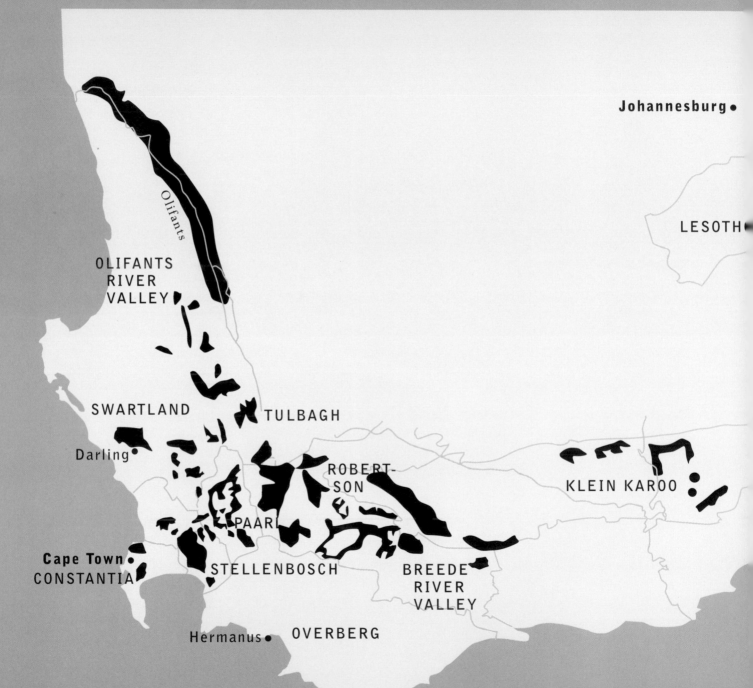

Johannesburg

LESOTH

Olifants

OLIFANTS
RIVER
VALLEY

SWARTLAND

TULBAGH

Darling

ROBERT-
SON

KLEIN KAROO

PAARL

Cape Town
CONSTANTIA

STELLENBOSCH

BREEDE
RIVER
VALLEY

Hermanus

OVERBERG

A decade ago, South African wines were rustic and rough around the edges, often even dull, but with post-Apartheid investment and new plantings of international varieties, things are definitely improving.

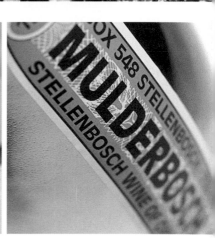

MAJOR RED GRAPES

Pinotage, Cabernet Sauvignon, Merlot, Shiraz, Pinot Noir.

MAJOR WHITE GRAPES

Sauvignon Blanc, Chardonnay, Chenin Blanc, Colombard.

KEY PRODUCERS

Hamilton Russell, Vergelegen, Rustenberg, Klein Constantia, Groot Constantia, Fairview, Kanonkop, Meerlust, Stellenbosch Vineyards, Graham Beck, Mulderbosch, Nederburg, Saxenburg, Warwick, Raats, Jordan, Boekenhoutskloof, Flagstone, Boschendal, Steenburg, Rust en Vrede, Kumala.

WINES TO LOOK FOR

Pinotage is South Africa's "national grape," making big, intense reds.

FINE VINTAGES

1991, 1992, 1993, 1995, 1997, 1998, 2001, 2002, 2003.

TIP

Don't be put off South African wines just because you don't like Pinotage. It is an acquired taste, but there are plenty of other juicy, ripe reds to choose from, notably the new "Cape Blend."

SOUTH AFRICA

The wine-growing regions of South Africa are among the most beautiful in the world, with the finest being clustered at the southern tip of the country, in the Cape. Wine has been made here for almost 350 years, vines first planted by early Dutch settlers.

The best-known region is Stellenbosch, home to fine quality, full-flavored reds made from Cabernet Sauvignon, Shiraz, and Merlot and an increasing number of elegant Sauvignon Blancs. South African producers have been quick to exploit the enormous potential of wine tourism, and Stellenbosch is the perfect region to visit, with its awe-inspiring scenery, fine wines, and welcoming wineries.

There are similar quality reds made from Shiraz and Cabernet Sauvignon to be found in Paarl, Franschhoek, and Wellington, while cool climate Walker Bay is becoming famous for its subtle Pinot Noirs and classy Chardonnays.

Until recently, the vast majority of South African wines were white, but red wine production is catching up and it is now almost half and half. Hitherto, the most important varieties have been the red Pinotage (South Africa's "own" grape, grown nowhere else) and the white Chenin Blanc. Pinotage has its devotees, but for many, its characteristic "burned rubber" is too much of an acquired taste. More user-friendly examples are being made, and in an effort to please consumers without losing their wine traditions, producers have come up with the "Cape Blend." This blends a minimum 20 percent Pinotage with Cabernet Sauvignon, Cabernet Franc, Merlot, and Shiraz. These latter varieties are proving popular in their own right, however, not just as part of this blend.

South African wines are not expensive, and for many they fall into the "good bargain" category. But, at long last, some top class wines are also being produced (priced accordingly) and there is now much to tempt the connoisseur.

Soon it will be easier to list those countries that do not produce wine than those that do. Changes in climate, improvements in technology, and increased investment have resulted in more countries making quality wine than would have been thought possible 20 years ago.

OTHER AREAS

Outside the countries that we have already considered, Algeria, Austria, Belgium, Bolivia, Bulgaria, Brazil, China, Croatia, Cyprus, Czech Republic, England, Georgia, Greece, Hungary, India, Israel, Japan, Lebanon, Luxembourg, Malta, Mexico, Moldova, Morocco, Peru, Romania, Slovakia, Slovenia, Switzerland, Tunisia, Turkey, and Uruguay all make wine of varying degrees of palatability.

AUSTRIA

Most of Austria's wine production is white and most of it is consumed domestically. The wines most often seen abroad are the world-class dessert wines produced on the banks of the Neusiedlersee in Burgenland. At their best, these are spectacular and make a fascinating alternative to those of Germany or France.

ENGLAND & WALES

The wines of England and Wales are constantly improving. The soil and climate of southern England are not dissimilar to those of Champagne, and sparkling wines made by the *méthode traditionelle* from Chardonnay and Pinot Noir can be especially good. "English Wine" is the term given to wine made in England and Wales from grapes grown there, while "British Wine" is the term given to wine made in Britain from imported grape juice.

GREECE

Greece's wines have taken on a new lease of life, proving that it can produce more than just that classic example of an acquired taste—Retsina. The indigenous grape varieties are utterly impossible to spell or pronounce, but they produce some fine punchy reds and aromatic whites that are increasingly memorable.

HUNGARY

Hungary is responsible for a lot of undistinguished table wine (the best-known of which is the full-bodied red called Bull's Blood), but is justly celebrated as the home of one of the world's finest wines, Tokaji. This sumptuous sweet wine is made from botrytis-affected grapes, the most important of which is Furmint, also now being used to make new-wave dry wines.

LEBANON

It amazes many that Lebanon is able to grow wine at all, especially given that almost all the vineyards are in the war-ravaged Bekaa Valley. The grape varieties are nearly all French, and the best wines are red, and the best of these really are very good indeed.

SWITZERLAND

Most of Switzerland's wine production is drunk by the Swiss themselves, although visiting tourists on skiing trips have been known to make pretty fair inroads. There are some light and fruity reds made from Pinot Noir and Gamay, but most wines are white, chiefly made from Chasselas, Switzerland's own grape.

KEY PRODUCERS AUSTRIA

Lenz Moser, Willi Opitz, FX Pichler, Bründlmayer, Kracher, Nikolaihof.

KEY PRODUCERS ENGLAND & WALES

Nyetimber, Breaky Bottom, Ridgeview, Denbies, Three Choirs, Sharpham.

KEY PRODUCERS GREECE

Gaia, Boutari, Kyr-Yianni, Sigalas, Biblia Chora.

KEY PRODUCERS HUNGARY

Royal Tokaji Wine Co., Oremus, István Szepsy.

KEY PRODUCERS LEBANON

Ch. Musar, Ch. Ksara, Ch. Kefraya.

KEY PRODUCERS SWITZERLAND

Guido Brivio, Baumann Weingut, Les Perrières, Les Frères Dubois.

DESSERT &
FORTIFIED

SWEET WINES

The world's most celebrated dessert wines come from Sauternes and Barsac in Bordeaux, and from Germany and Hungary, although fine examples are also produced in Alsace, Austria, Australia, California, Canada, and Greece.

A dessert wine can be sweet for a number of reasons: it might be a "late-picked" wine, known in France as Vendange Tardive, made from extremely ripe grapes picked late in the season when their sweetness is most concentrated; it might be the even more exotic Sélection de Grains Nobles, picked berry by berry; or it might be a Vin Doux Naturel such as Muscat de Beaumes-de-Venise, whose fermentation has been stopped by the addition of distilled grape spirit before all the sugar has turned to alcohol.

Alternatively, like a Sauternes or Barsac, it might have been made from grapes affected by noble rot, the name given to *Botrytis Cinerea*—known as *pourriture noble* in France and *edelfäule* in Germany. Botrytis is a beneficial mold which, in areas prone to damp, humid conditions, attacks certain grapes absorbing their moisture content, making them shrivel and rot, thus concentrating their flavor and their sugars. Sauvignon Blanc, Sémillon, Chenin Blanc, and Gewurztraminer in France, and Riesling in Germany are particularly susceptible to this, and, the grapes having been picked individually by hand, produce dessert wines high in alcohol and richness of flavor. It is a laborious and wasteful process, however, for while a single vine is capable of producing a bottle of ordinary wine, it will only produce one glass of Sauternes.

Desserts are often greatly improved by an accompanying glass of dessert wine—a German Trockenbeerenauslese perhaps, or a sweet Vouvray, a California Black Muscat, or an Australian Orange Muscat and Flora. But beware, eating some fruits can make such wines taste less sweet than usual, and chocolate in particular is a tricky partner for wine, having a tendency to overwhelm even the greatest of dessert wines. But don't feel you have to keep the Sauternes, Barsac, or Muscat de Beaumes-de-Venise for just the desserts: do as the French do, and drink them well-chilled with rich hors d'oeuvres such as pâté de foie gras.

STYLE

Rich, luscious, voluptuous, sweet.

GOES WITH

Foie gras, blue cheese, desserts.

FAMOUS DESSERT WINES

Ch. d'Yquem, Ch. Climens, Ch. Rieussec (Sauternes and Barsac). Royal Tokaji Wine Co. Tokaji Eszencia (Hungary), Inniskillin Ice wine (Canada), Andrew Quady Elysium Black Muscat (California).

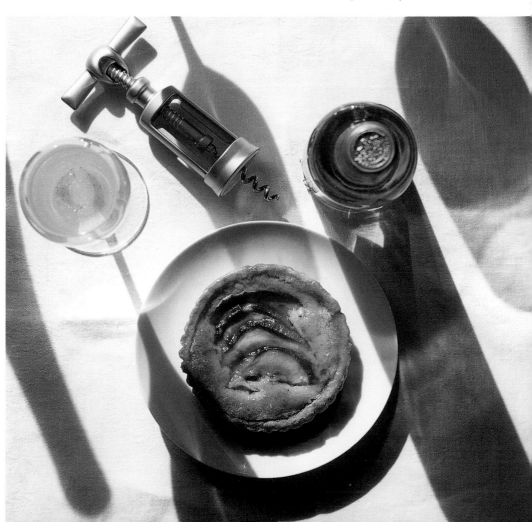

STYLE

Sweet, ranging from soft, mellow, "Tawny," to intense, heady "Vintage."

GOES WITH

Stilton and other blue cheeses or, best of all, on its own.

FAMOUS PORTS

Quinta do Noval, Taylor's, Dow's, Warre's, Graham's.

PORT

Port is produced from grapes grown in vineyards situated along the River Douro in northern Portugal. The town from which the wine takes its name, Porto, lies at the river's mouth. It is here that the newly blended wines are brought to mature in the lodges of neighboring Vila Nova de Gaia.

Up to 18 different grape varieties are permitted to be used in blending port, the most important of which is Touriga Nacional. The final product is made by adding distilled grape spirit to partially fermented red wine, thus stopping its fermentation and leaving the wine sweet, rich, and high in alcohol.

There are many types of port, but in essence they fall into two categories: those that are matured in wood, and those that are matured in bottle. Tawny (or wood) ports are blended wines that spend anything from 10–40 years maturing in cask before bottling, by which stage they are ready for immediate consumption. The sediment is left in the barrel so no decanting is required. They make excellent companions to fruit cakes and cookies, and are the new fashionable accompaniment, chilled, with chocolate desserts.

Vintage port is made only in exceptional years and only from the best grapes harvested from the best vineyards. It spends two years in wood before being bottled, after which it can take up to 20 years to mature, then remains at its peak for another 20 years before spending the next 20 years in a gentle decline. By the time vintage port is ready to drink, it will have a sediment and will thus need to be decanted. Port producers decide by consensus whether or not a particular year is good enough to be "declared" as a Vintage.

There are other hybrid forms of port such as Vintage Character (a blend of good quality ports from several vintages, aged in cask for about five years before being bottled), Crusted (a blend of different years that spends between three to four years in cask before completing its maturation in bottle), and Late Bottled Vintage (port from a single year, that is not quite up to full-blown Vintage quality, that is aged in cask for up to six years).

The recent declared port vintages are 1980, 1982, 1983, 1985, 1991, 1992, 1994, 1997, 1998, 2000. In some years a vintage might not be considered as important and will be declared by a few port houses only, as Single Quinta port.

ABOVE LEFT SYMINGTON FAMILY ESTATES, PORTUGAL.

STYLE

Range from tangy, dry Manzanilla through medium-dry Amontillado to rich and intense Oloroso.

GOES WITH

Dry sherry makes a great aperitif or accompaniment to tapas and simple soups. Sweet sherry is ideal with icecream or after a meal.

FAMOUS SHERRIES

Lustau, Barbadillo, Gomez, Hidalgo, Harveys, González Byass.

SHERRY

Sherry comes from the deep southwest corner of Spain, taking its name from the town of Jerez de la Frontera. It is a fortified white wine made from Moscatel, Palomino, and Pedro Ximénez grapes fermented in barrels above ground (rather than in cellars) and coming in a wide variety of styles and flavors.

Once fermented, and then fortified, the barrels of wine are categorized dependent upon their aging potential. The new wine is added to a line of anything up to 100 butts known as the solera—a system that involves the topping up of older barrels with younger wine of the same style ensuring that it always tastes the same—while fully mature wine ready for blending comes out of the other end. Although the wines are usually sold under brand names, the label will also state what style of sherry it is. The appetizingly salty Manzanilla, which comes from Jerez's neighbouring town of Sanlúcar de Barrameda, and Fino are the driest sherries, whose zip and freshness make them great kick-starters for the appetite. Sanlúcar and Jerez have a unique microclimate, which leads to a film of yeast, known as "flor," growing on the surface of the sherry: this gives Fino and Manzanilla their individual tangy flavor.

Amontillado is effectively an aged Fino, whose time spent in cask imparts a medium-dry nuttiness. Pale Cream is a sweetened Fino and Cream is the sweeter still. Both these wines tend to lack the richness and fullness of flavor to be found in a top-class Oloroso, (a fully oxidized sherry) which can be dry or sweet to the taste. Pedro Ximénex (or PX) is an intensely sweet, gloopy, tar-colored sherry that makes an intriguing and delectable after-dinner drink.

MADEIRA

The fortified wine madeira comes from the Portuguese island of that name that lies some 400 miles off the coast of Morocco. During the 18th century, the indifferent wine produced here was often used as ballast on long sea voyages, during which it was found that the double crossing of the Equator greatly reduced the wine's acidic mediocrity and allowed a period of maturation that vastly improved its flavor. Nowadays the fermented wine is effectively "cooked" to replicate the heat of the sea voyages before it is fortified.

There are four types of madeira, ranging from very dry to very sweet: Sercial, Verdelho, Bual, and Malmsey. The driest of the madeiras goes well with soups, the slightly sweeter ones with cookies, while the richest of all go excellently with old-fashioned, very sweet desserts such as treacle tart and steamed syrup pudding.

Madeira may seem old-fashioned, but it is making a comeback, and is far too enjoyable to be drunk only at Christmas.

NEW WORLD FORTIFIED

Australia, California, and South Africa all produce excellent fortified wines from a variety of grapes, Rutherglen in Victoria being especially celebrated for its intense liqueur Muscats. For years, such wines were looked down upon in Europe as poor imitations of port (with many being marketed as "Port"), although today they are finally being appreciated for being fine wines in their own right. Although port's main grape, Touriga Nacional, is sometimes used, so, too are Cabernet Sauvignon, Zinfandel, Petite Sirah, and, especially in Australia, Muscat, and Tokay (or Muscadelle).

STYLE

Dry to sweet, with delicious notes of toast, nuts, and raisins.

GOES WITH

Ideal aperitif, mid-morning sharpener, or digestif.

FAMOUS MADEIRA

Madeira Wine Company, Vinho Barbeita.

MAKING THE MOST OF EVERY GLASS

The range of wine styles and flavors grows

with each successive vintage; glassware

becomes ever more elegant and sophisticated;

technology is leading us from cork closures

to screwcaps; food-and-wine pairing engages

us all. It is a good time to be a wine lover.

CHOOSING WINE BY STYLE

The range of wine is today so vast and varied that there is something to suit every possible taste. But don't just stick with one you like, keep experimenting. You don't have to spend a fortune and you can always use the lesser wines in cooking.

SPARKLING WINES

Fine champagne has a knack of making one feel good about oneself in a way that no other drink can—with the possible exception of a perfectly made dry martini—whereas bad champagne can be alarmingly raw and acidic, seemingly able to strip the enamel

from your teeth. The trouble is that the word "champagne" on a label guarantees the wine's geographical origin (except in the U.S.), the method of production, and the grape varieties used, not its quality. Other sparkling wine, however good, may not have quite the same panache (after all, one talks of a champagne lifestyle rather than a sparkling wine lifestyle, and of champagne bars rather than sparkling wine bars) but there are some stunning ones around and they should not be dismissed.

Of the cheaper sparkling wines, Cava springs immediately to mind, but with its reputation

for housing a headache in every bottle, care must be taken to search out good examples. Better instead to search out a fine French sparkler such as to Blanquette de Limoux, a sparkling Vouvray or Clairette de Die, an Italian Asti, or Prosecco, or a German Sekt. Or look to the New World: Australia, New Zealand, and California in particular are producing some remarkable sparkling wines, usually made by the *méthode traditionelle* from the same champagne grapes as used in Champagne, and often in conjunction with some of the finest Champagne houses who have invested heavily in those regions.

LIGHT WHITE WINES

Most of us enjoy a light, drinkable white wine and many of us started our drinking careers on your average Liebfraumilch or the like. Nobody should be criticized for starting with such wines; what is inexcusable is not having moved on.

Although German Rieslings are often unfairly tarred with the Liebfraumilch brush, these can be really classy. There is a trend to make such wines slightly drier and more alcoholic than of old, but you can still find clean, pure Riesling from the Mosel, say, which are slightly off-dry and refreshingly light in alcohol: as little as seven percent in some cases. Other fine Rieslings are made in Alsace, Chile, Australia, New Zealand, South Africa, and California.

Other wines that provide light, floral, and easy-drinking include the Italian Orvieto (which can be dry or off-dry), Frascati, Soave, or Pinot Grigio. The newly trendy Albariño from Rías Baixas in Spain, is delightfully drinkable, and the simple wines from the Loire, such as Muscadet or Vouvray or the wines from Côtes de Gascogne in France's southwest are also worth searching out.

GRASSY WHITES

For light wines that have a bit more character and elegance, try the aristocratic Sauvignon Blancs from the Loire such as Pouilly-Fumé and Sancerre. These are bone dry, but have wonderful aromas of cut grass. For Sauvignons with a bit more of a flashy edge to them, try the exuberant wines of New Zealand or Chile, jam-packed with gooseberry and nettle aromas and tropical flavors.

FULL-BODIED AND OAKY WHITES

New World Chardonnay, especially from Australia or California, is now many people's entry point to wine, and it is in this category that the New World really gets into its stride. But Chardonnay is more than just up-front and in-yer-face. Indeed, if you were so minded, you could drink nothing but Chardonnay and never be bored, so varied are the styles.

Don't fall into the trap of thinking that all Chardonnay tastes like Australian Chardonnay. Try some white burgundy such as top quality Côte de Beaune like Meursault, Puligny-Montrachet, or even the mighty Corton-Charlemagne (if you can afford it). Or the less grand, but eminently reliable Montagny and Rully from the Côte Chalonnaise, or Pouilly-Fuissé, St. Véran, and Mâcon-Lugny from the Mâconnais. If you want your Chardonnays to be flintier, steelier, and more austere, then go for the wines of Chablis, many of which don't go near an oak barrel, or those from Italy's Alto Adige.

Other big whites to look out for include white Rhônes, such as the Marsanne-Roussanne-based Hermitage, or Condrieu made from the currently fashionable Viognier, which can be oily and buttery. Also keep an eye out for the aromatic, smoky Pinot Gris and absurdly flamboyant, rich, and spicy Gewurztraminers of Alsace. Both these grapes are grown successfully around the world, but never quite reach the opulent heights they do here. If you like them a bit more *piano*, try the Italian versions.

RICH OR SWEET WHITES

Sweet wines are one of life's greatest pleasures and they can be drunk on their own, with rich first courses, desserts, or stinky cheeses. For real lip-smacking sweeties, go to Hungary for its unique Tokaji, redolent of honey and marmalade, to Alsace for the late-picked Gewurztraminers, to Germany for its sumptuous late-picked or botrytised Trocken-beerenauslese Rieslings, and to Austria for the great sweet wines from the town of Rust on the misty Neusiedlersee. In France, the great Sauvignon Blanc/Sémillon sweet wines come from Sauternes and Barsac in Bordeaux, and from St. Croix du Mont. Chenin Blanc is all honey and nuts when used to make the dessert wines of Coteaux du Layon and Vouvray.

In the New World, California and Australia, in particular, produce some strikingly good sweet wines, mainly from Muscat and other rather more obscure varieties. And if you get a chance, try a bottle of Canadian Icewine, made from grapes picked while still frozen on the vine and truly one of the wine world's most seductive treats.

LIGHT AND FRUITY REDS

There are hundreds of inexpensive, non-vintage blended and branded wines (wines marketed by a brand name that doesn't come from a particular place) around. When you find one you enjoy, work out what it is about it that you like and then move on into the wine world proper. Among the best examples of light red wines with plenty of juicy fruit, which can be drunk with or without food, are those made from Gamay such as Beaujolais or Gamay de Touraine from the Loire. The young wine of Beaujolais, Beaujolais Nouveau, has something of a poor reputation and even the best examples struggle to be taken seriously: but they are undemanding wines which are best drunk young without much ceremony and (shock horror) can benefit from being chilled.

If you are a Beaujolais fan, other light, fruity, and vibrant reds that you might enjoy are the Cabernet Franc wines of the Loire Valley such as Chinon or Bourgueil, Italian reds such as Valpolicella and Bardolino, and the hard to find—but hugely enjoyable—Pinot Noirs from Germany, Austria, and Alsace.

SOFT, MELLOW, OR MEDIUM-BODIED REDS

Top quality, oak-aged Rioja is famous for its mellow softness and warm, seductive aromas of cherry fruit and vanilla. Mature Pinot Noir from Burgundy has the less appetising-sounding bouquet of the farmyard and rotting vegetables, but it is actually delicious and highly prized by connoisseurs. For early drinking and more fruity examples, go to Burgundy's Côte Chalonnaise for wines such as Mercurey, Rully and Givry and, for wines that need more time, the Côte de Nuits and its Gevrey-Chambertin, Morey-St-Denis, and Nuits St-Georges or the Côte de Beaune for Beaune, Pommard, Volnay, and Aloxe-Corton.

Cabernet Sauvignon can produce big, powerful wines or wines of notable subtlety and elegance, especially when blended with a dash of Merlot. For soft and mellow examples, try lesser-known St. Emilions from Bordeaux or those under-rated wines of the Côte de Bourg and the Côte de Blaye.

Côtes du Rhône, Crozes-Hermitage, and Côte Rôtie (which has a small amount of the white grape, Viognier, added to it) are all good examples from the Rhône, but try Chianti or other Sangiovese wines from Italy, too, and cool climate New World reds such as New Zealand Merlot or Pinot Noir, or Pinot Noir from Oregon.

JUICY, FRUIT-FORWARD, FULL-BODIED REDS

For the jammier and fuller-bodied reds, oak-aged Merlot or Cabernet Sauvignon from California or Chile are ideal, as are California Pinot Noirs. These wines tend to be fuller than many European ones thanks to a more constant, warm climate. But try, too, the top-class, silky wines from Margaux or St. Emilion in Bordeaux, and the slightly more earthy St. Estèphes or Pessac-Léognans. Or explore the increasingly sophisticated Portuguese reds made from the port grape Touriga Nacional.

BIG, POWERFUL, OR SPICY REDS

The best in this category come from the New World, where a hot climate and a tendency to go for single varietals results in some massively full-flavored wines, often with a commensurately high alcohol content. Zinfandel from California (the proper, spicy red ones, not the ghastly, off-dry pink ones) and Pinotage from South Africa are obvious choices, as are the meaty Shirazes from Australia—some unblended, some mixed with Cabernet Sauvignon or Merlot. You need a knife and fork for some of these. Argentinian and Chilean wines made from such varieties as Tannat and Malbec are worth seeking out, too.

In the Old World, top Hermitage and Cornas from the Northern Rhône, or Châteauneuf-du-Pape and Gigonas from the Southern Rhône can be strapping wines, or try other body-building French wines such as Cahors or Bandol. In northwest Italy, Barbaresco and Barolo, both made from Nebbiolo, are dark and intense and need plenty of aging to soften the tannins. The strong and powerful Amarone shouldn't be overlooked, either.

ROSES

Rosés are becoming increasingly popular and should provide easy-drinking par excellence. Off-dry rosés like white Zinfandel, Rosé d'Anjou, or the Portuguese Mateus Rosé don't enhance the wines' image, but the best rosés are good, if rarely excellent. Fuller-bodied examples from southern France—Lirac, Provencal rosé, and Tavel—or those made from Garnacha in Spain's Rioja and Navarra are well-worth summer-glugging. Some Bordeaux rosés are also good.

FORTIFIED WINES

Port, sherry, and madeira are the most famous of all fortified wines, but there are some fine alternatives, such as the lusciously sweet Vin Doux Naturals from southern France, such as Muscat de Beaumes-de-Venise or Banyuls, and the utterly delicious liqueur Muscats from Australia and South Africa.

BOTTLES & LABELS

BOTTLES

The regular wine bottle is standardized the world over at 75 cl. (about five or six glasses). Other sizes, such as half-bottles (37 cl.), liter bottles (100 cl.), and magnums (150 cl.) are also often seen. The general rule of thumb is that the larger the bottle, the more slowly the wine within it will mature—and the longer it will keep—owing to the ratio of wine to oxygen in the bottle.

In this age of designer chic, European wine producers are sticking less strictly to the traditionally-shaped bottles of their respective regions, whilst producers from the New World are divided between those who use the shapes most associated with each particular variety and those who bottle their wines in whatever shape pleases them. Nevertheless, the shape and color of a wine bottle remain useful tools for identifying the style and type of wine inside.

There are basically three different shapes for table wine: Bordeaux style—green with high shoulders; Burgundy style—greeny-brown with sloping shoulders; and Germanic—tall and slender, in green or brown.

As well as red and white Bordeaux, Californian and Australian varietals such as Cabernet Sauvignon, Merlot, and Shiraz, come in Bordeaux style bottles, as do Zinfandels, Chianti, and some Riojas. New World Sauvignon Blancs and Sémillons come in this shape, too, in either green or clear glass.

As well as Burgundy and Rhône wines, both red and white, Beaujolais, Californian Pinot Noir, big Italians such as Barolo and Barbaresco, Syrah, and some Spanish wines come in Burgundy-style bottles. New World Chardonnays also tend to appear in this style.

The aromatic wines of Alsace, Germany, and beyond come in tall, slender bottles. Those from Alsace are green, whereas German wines have an additional distinction, in that wines from the Mosel (known as Moselles) usually come in green bottles and those from the Rhine (known as Hocks) come in brown bottles, although this distinction is becoming blurred.

Apart from a couple of rare exceptions, champagne and other sparkling wines come in dark green bottles with sloping shoulders and a pronounced indentation in the base—a punt. Champagne producers are famous for using over-sized bottles for their wines:

- Magnum = 2 bottles
- Jeroboam = 4 bottles
- Rehoboam = 6 bottles
- Methuselah = 8 bottles
- Salmanazar = 12 bottles
- Balthazar = 16 bottles
- Nebuchadnezzar = 20 bottles

Récolte

BARBE RAC ®

Châteauneuf-du-

APPELLATION CHÂTEAUNEUF-DU-PAPE CONTRO

Mis en bouteille par M. CHAPOUTIER

Red wine - Vin rouge

Produit de France - Product of France

LABELS

In essence, wine labels are no different from baked beans or instant coffee labels: they are there to give you all the information you need to decide whether or not to buy the product.

As a rule, New World producers market their wines by grape variety, while the Europeans tend not to (although this is changing) so it helps to know which varieties make which wines.

While front labels are strictly regulated, back labels (an optional extra) often give a fuller explanation of the wine. Neck labels are sometimes added, stating the vintage, some special feature about the wine, or displaying an award won.

A wine label on the front or back of a bottle must, legally, tell you:

- the wine's name, possibly including the grape variety
- the size of the bottle
- the vintage (if there is one)
- the wine's alcoholic strength
- the producer's name and address
- the name of the bottler (if different from the producer)
- the name of the shipper (if different from the importer)
- the name of the importer
- the wine's quality level
- where the wine was bottled
- country of origin
- type of wine
- what region and appellation the wine is from

Wine imported into the United States, or exported from there, is also obliged to state whether or not sulphur dioxide was used in its production, and to display a government health warning concerning the hazards of drinking wine. (If only the French or Italians would consider displaying a similar label extolling the benefits.)

Of all white wines, those from Germany have the most perplexing labels, not only because they are often written in indecipherable Gothic script, but also because they use terms that categorize the ripeness (therefore sweetness) of the grapes. Kabinett is the driest level of quality wine, followed by Spätlese, Auslese, Beerenauslese, and Trockenbeerenauslese.

QUALITY CLASSIFICATIONS

Wine laws are strict and their purpose is two-fold: to protect the producer, by ensuring that his region's reputation isn't undermined, and the consumer, by guaranteeing the basic quality and character of the wine.

Virtually every European wine-growing region has its own rules as to which grapes may be used, and where and by what method they might be grown and vinified. New World wines are not subject to such strict restrictions, something that is often compensated for by producers giving extraordinarily detailed information on the back label. This might change, however, as in 1983 the United States set up the American Viticultural Area (AVA) system, in an attempt to emulate France's AOC laws, and other non-EU countries may follow suit.

In general, France's stringent Appellation d'Origine Contrôlée (AOC) laws give a guarantee as to a wine's origins and authenticity as to grape variety, but without guaranteeing quality. The categories below AOC are VDQS (Vin Délimité de Qualité Supérieure), Vin de Pays, and Vin de Table: these are for lower quality wines and have less rigid restrictions as to their production.

In Burgundy, a classification of Premiers Crus and Grands Crus identifies the best vineyards, based on location, while Alsace contains elements of both systems.

Italy has a similar system to France, the Denominazione di Origine Controllata (DOC), although many top producers consider it too restrictive and make great wines that are obliged to be classified as only Vino da Tavola. A more recent classification, Indicazione Geografica Tipica (IGT) has been introduced to alleviate some of the confusion.

Unlike France, Spain and Italy designate their wines Reserva/Riserva to indicate a certain period in oak, a treatment usually confined to only the best wines.

WHERE TO BUY

The differences between traditional wine merchants and supermarkets (where almost 70 percent of customers buy their wine) are becoming more and more blurred. Supermarkets are encouraging their staff to become better informed, and high-end wine shops are setting up online stores on the Web.

DEDICATED WINE SHOPS

The advantages: You will get unrivaled advice and personal service from real wine lovers. Imaginative offerings will reflect the owner's own enthusiasms and will invariably be from top-class producers, many of whom produce too little to be stocked by the supermarkets or, grocery stores, or liquor stores. You will have the chance to buy *"en primeur"* (at the opening price for the wine, before it has even been bottled) and to store your purchases in temperature-controled cellars. There will be older vintages available and the chance to enjoy "try before you buy" tastings. And, if nothing else, there is always the upscale packaging.
The disadvantages: Advice from seemingly well-informed experts costs money, as does the stylish packaging, and for every true enthusiast behind the counter, there is often someone whose knowledge leaves much to be desired.

GROCERY STORES AND LIQUOR STORES

The advantages: Usually highly convenient, next door to the Chinese takeout or around the corner from your friend's house. The best examples have dedicated, well-informed (and often charmingly eccentric) staff who are generally rather less intimidating than staff in high-end wine shops. There are always special offers and a large range of chilled wines for impulsive purchases, as well as beers, liquor, and cigarettes.
The disadvantages: The worst examples have store managers who wouldn't know the difference between a Cabernet or a Kabinett and the chilled wines only ever seem to be White Zinfandel and the like. The range of wines is dependent on store size and can therefore be severely limited, and will usually be for immediate drinking only.

SUPERMARKETS

The advantages: The awesome buying power of the supermarkets results in some wonderful bargains, added to which the major wine distributors regularly spend vast sums buying market share through heavy discounts. You can combine your wine buying with the weekly shopping and do your food-and-wine matching on the hoof.

The disadvantages: The wines have to cater for everyone, from the heat-and-serve slurper to the budding gourmet, and there are rarely examples of the truly spectacular wines available. Information and advice can be rare and the huge volume sales prohibit selling small producers' wines. As a result, consistency of stock can be irritatingly patchy.

MAIL ORDER/INTERNET

The advantages: This can be ridiculously convenient, depending on where you live. The Internet in particular, offers limitless information on the wines, with regular special offers and door-to-door delivery.

The disadvantages: There are many restrictions to ordering wine by mail order or the Internet. Only 14 states currently allow wine shipments from out-of-state, while some won't allow in-state shipments either. See www.wineinstitute.org for detailed information. In adddition, deliveries can go astray and special offers often turn out to be not very special. There is no opportunity to try the wines first and you usually have to buy in quantity, necessitating space to store at home. Definitely not for the spontaneous drinker.

BUYING AT AUCTION

The advantages: This is wine-buying with added theater. Amazing bargains are there for the asking and auctions are an excellent source of fully mature burgundies, clarets and ports. Bids can be placed in person, online, or by mail.

The disadvantages: This really is a case of "buyer beware." The wines on sale might have been poorly stored or have dubious provenance and it is all too easy to have a rush of blood to the head and end up with a 10 year supply of cooking wine. There are many extras that need to be taken into consideration, such as buyers' commission, tax, and delivery charges, all of which can make your purchase seem less of a bargain.

PUTTING TOGETHER A CELLAR

It has never been easier to buy wine. Ordinary reds, whites, and sparkling wines can be bought when needed from supermarkets, retail chains, and wine merchants—but fully mature fine wine is both hard to find and often prohibitively expensive.

If you want to drink quality wine of some age, the only sensible option is to mature it yourself by laying it down. Wine for everyday drinking is not intended to be laid down— rather than maturing, it simply loses its fruit and vivacity. There is no point in cluttering up your cellar with wines that you can get easily and cheaply elsewhere or with wines that will not improve. Instead, seek out wines of quality, rarity, and aging potential.

Start by buying what you like to drink. You need also to decide whether your wines are for consumption or investment, or both. Some smart wine lovers buy two cases of each wine, one to drink and one to sell. This way, after the initial investment, a cellar can become self-financing. Keep up-to-date with what's happening in the world of wine by joining suppliers' mailing lists, looking on the Internet, and reading magazines such as *Wine & Spirits* and *Wine Spectator*, as well as newspaper wine columns.

Consistent and favorable climates in the Americas, Australasia, and South Africa, and increasingly sophisticated technology in Europe's wine-growing areas mean that really poor vintages are a thing of the past, but there can still be huge variations between years, and age alone does not define a good wine. Don't buy wine from just one vintage or your cellar will lack variety, and you may find that the style of a subsequent vintage is more to your taste. Remember, too, that different vintages age at different rates, and that later vintages are sometimes ready to drink before earlier ones.

Tastes and budgets differ, and no two cellars will be alike, but a notional well-balanced cellar might include several bottles of Cabernet and Merlot, red and white burgundy and Rhône for the long term, plus a couple of bottles of vintage champagne and vintage port and some half-bottles of dessert wine. For the short term, there might be some white wines from the Loire and some mid-range wines from California, Chile, or New Zealand.

CABERNET SAUVIGNON AND MERLOT

Top-quality wines made from Cabernet Sauvignon demand to be laid down, whether they are the finest single varietals from California, Australia, Chile, and Italy, or the subtle blended wines from Bordeaux known as clarets. Wines made from Merlot also merit time in the cellar, although they will mature more quickly than their Cabernet counterparts.

PINOT NOIR

Although Pinot Noir ages well, its most sought-after wines, such as those from New Zealand, Oregon, and Burgundy, are now usually made for early consumption. Investing in burgundy can be both simple and confusing: simple because all red burgundies are made from one grape—Pinot Noir—and confusing because wines of the same name but from different producers proliferate. It is vital, therefore, either to get to know names of producers you like or to find a specialized supplier whom you trust.

SYRAH, GRENACHE, & ZINFANDEL

Wines made from Syrah—also known as Shiraz—and from Grenache are ideal to lay down. Both varieties produce wines of great power, with abundant fruit and plenty of tannin, perfect for lengthy maturation. The best examples are the blockbuster Shirazes from Australia and the Syrah-based Northern Rhônes and the Grenache-based Southern Rhônes from France, all of which are much prized by collectors. Keep an eye out, too, for the best California Zinfandels.

CHARDONNAY & VIOGNIER

Chardonnay is the best of all white grape varieties to lay down. Choose the finest examples from Australia, California, Burgundy, and Chablis. Oak-aged Chardonnay, in particular, matures well, taking on deep yellow hues and rich toasty and buttery aromas as the years pass. Serious wines made from Viognier are also worth making space for in your cellar.

SAUVIGNON BLANC

As a rule, wines made from Sauvignon Blanc do not age well—if kept for too long, they lose their zest. Notable exceptions are the powerful dessert wines blended from Sauvignon Blanc and Sémillon, which benefit from lengthy storage. For short-term cellaring, have some good-quality California or New Zealand Sauvignons or some Sancerres or Pouilly-Fumés from the Loire.

CHAMPAGNE & SPARKLING WINES

Vintage champagne (made in exceptional years only) is ideal for maturing, as are the finest New World sparkling wines made from the classic Chardonnay/Pinot Noir/Pinot Meunier blend. Good-quality non-vintage champagne (produced every year) can be laid down over a couple of years to let its acidity soften and mellow.

DESSERT WINE

Dessert wines are well worth keeping, be they the great Sauvignon/Sémillon blends of Sauternes and Barsac, the intense Riesling Trockenbeerenausleses of Germany, the sumptuous Vendanges Tardives of Alsace, or the unique Tokajis of Hungary. A little dessert wine goes a long way, so buy it in half-bottles.

PORT

There are two main types of port, wood and vintage. Wood port is aged in cask; since it is mature once bottled there is no point in cellaring it. Vintage port is made only three or four times a decade and spends only a short time in cask before lengthy maturation in bottle. This is the type of port to lay down.

MISCELLANEOUS

Other wines to consider are top Riojas from Spain, Italy's super *vini da tavola*, Chianti, and hefty wines such as Barolo and Barbaresco, and Australia and California are producing full-bodied red wines and big Chardonnays and Semillions that repay keeping.

SHERRY, MADEIRA, & SPIRITS

Fino and manzanilla sherries must be drunk promptly to enjoy their zippy freshness, but olorosos can develop a pleasing nuttiness over time. Dry madeira can be used as an aperitif and sweet madeira as a digestif, and bottles won't spoil once opened. There is no point in storing spirits—however grand or illustrious a bottle of brandy or single malt whisky might be, it won't improve with age.

Bottles of wine are like babies— seemingly fragile and vulnerable, they are much more sturdy and resilient than you might imagine.

STORING WINE

There are three main options available to the wine collector: to store wine with the supplier from whom the wine was bought, to store wine at an independent wine warehouse, and to store wine at home. You don't need a cellar as such, simply comandeer a corner or cubby hole and fill it with bottles.

STORING WITH A SUPPLIER
The chief advantages of storing wine with a supplier are that suppliers offer excellent advice and the wine will be stored in perfect conditions in temperature-controlled cellars (out of temptation's way). The wine will also be easier to sell, should you wish to part with it, because auction houses and prospective buyers can be sure that it has been well kept. The disadvantages are that rental charges can be expensive and that you have to plan well in advance what you are going to drink and when.

STORING IN A WINE WAREHOUSE
Storing in a warehouse is similar to storing with a supplier, but you need to be sure that it is a reputable establishment and that both temperature and security are satisfactory. Check whether there are any charges for removal of stock, and confirm that they will deliver—some warehouses require customers to collect their wine. Bear in mind that you may be able to store and remove wine only by the unmixed case. Don't expect advice on what to drink when.

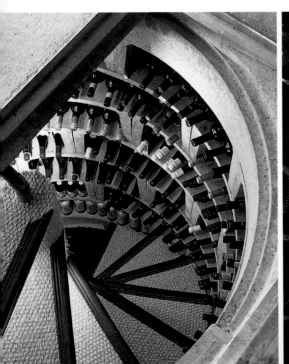

STORING AT HOME

When it comes to storage, wine falls into three broad categories: wine that needs time to mature (such as young top-quality claret, red burgundy, Sauternes, vintage champagne, and vintage port); wine that is unlikely to improve but which will keep (most mid-quality wine); and wine that needs to be drunk before it deteriorates (cheap wine or old top-quality wine). To make sure you drink your wine at its best—whatever the quality—it is vital that you look after it while it is in your care and remember a few simple rules.

- However many bottles you have, and whatever their quality, don't trust your memory. If you want to remember what you have bought, what you have drunk or given away, what you have enjoyed and what you haven't, what needs drinking up, what needs to be left alone, what items cost what, and what they are worth now, make a record of it.

- Always store wine on its side. This prevents the cork from drying out and shrinking. Leave the bottles of wine in their cardboard box and turn the box on its side. Fine wine in wooden cases should be left undisturbed: the bottles will already be lying flat, and, should you wish to sell them, unopened cases fetch a better price than opened ones.

- The larger the bottle, the longer the wine will take to mature and the longer it will keep, owing to the ratio of wine to air in the bottle.

- Keep wine at a constant temperature. Ideally, wine should be stored at 44–54°F, which is fine if you have the capability to control the temperature, but don't worry if you haven't—a constant temperature is far more important than the temperature itself, provided that it is within reasonable limits. Keep a max/min thermometer wherever you store your wine.

- Store wine away from movement, bright light, and strong smells. In other words, if you are storing wine (apart from everyday wine) for a length of time, keep it away from cooking areas, washing machines, elevator shafts, and garages: vibrations shake up the sediment, and the smell of fried onions or gas can be remarkably pervasive.

- If you intend to store your wine at home and don't have a genuine cellar, don't panic. You could use a study, guest room, or closet under the stairs. Alternatively, you might wish to invest in wine-storage cabinets or a spiral cellar.

- Wine-storage cabinets are self-contained, temperature-controlled units of varying size powered by electricity. The largest models are capable of storing up to 200 bottles. They can be used to store both red wines and white wines in separate compartments at serving temperature. The cabinets are usually faced in wood to blend in with domestic decor and furniture, but they take up a lot of space and need to be sited on a strong floor.

- Spiral cellars are ingenious contraptions. They may be expensive and awkward to install—and they are only suitable in places where there is enough room to maneuver—but they are wonderful and imaginative alternatives to having a more conventional wine cellar. Constructed from ready-made concrete tubes or steel, they are inserted into a large hole excavated beneath or near your home. Circulating around a spiral stairway are numerous niches into which bottles can be inserted. The concrete and the location are all that are needed to make sure temperature and humidity remain at the perfect level.

- Wherever you store your wine collection, don't forget to insure it—for the replacement value rather than just the purchase price.

GLASSES

You might think that wine would taste all right drunk from a (clean) coffee mug or that any old glass would do. But, if you are spending a considerable amount of money on some decent wine, it is worth taking the trouble to acquire glasses that will allow the wine to be enjoyed at its best. There is no need to be fussy but you will find that the right glass gives even the humblest wine a fighting chance.

glasses that are similar to each other but of different sizes: large for red and small for white. The glasses should have stems—so that your hands do not affect the wine's temperature or obscure its color and appearance—and the bowl of the glass should be slightly wider than the rim so that you can swirl the liquid around without spilling it and without losing the wine's aroma. Make sure your glasses are never more than half full: too much wine in the glass means there is no room for the aroma and bouquet to circulate.

• Plain, uncut, and uncolored glasses are ideal, giving the drinker a clear view of the wine. The better the glass, the lighter in weight it should be, and the easier to handle, enhancing the whole pleasure of wine.

• Dessert wines and fortified wines can be served in white wine glasses, although similar ones that are slightly smaller are better still.

Some wine lovers have a great array of glassware, even going as far as to have different glasses for different grape varieties, but for most of us that would be excessively punctilious. There is no need to spend a fortune—proper wine glasses are widely available and are not expensive. In an ideal world, it is good to have a choice of glasses for champagne and sparkling wines, white wines, red wines, and fortified wines.

The aroma and bouquet are vital elements of our enjoyment of a wine—because our

noses are infinitely more sensitive than our tongues—and that is where the style of glass has such a vital part to play.

• Champagne should be served in tall flutes whose tapering rim helps retain the sparkle that the winemaker has striven so hard to achieve. Wide-rimmed "saucers" should not be used, because these allow the bubbles to dissipate far too quickly.

• Red and white wine should be served in

• Make sure your glasses do not become tainted by tastes or smells that might affect the wine. Wash them after each use with a light detergent and dry them with a clean cloth, or rinse them in clear hot water and let them drip dry.

• Store your glasses upright in a closet, rather than face down, so that they don't get smells from the shelves trapped within them. Alternatively, hang them upside down from a rack.

EQUIPMENT

You may wish to make do with just a simple corkscrew, regarding other equipment as superfluous. But, if you have taken the trouble to buy some decent wine, it is worth stocking up on one or two other bits and pieces.

The number and quality of items of equipment and bar accessories that you decide to buy will depend upon how seriously you take the subject of wine.

- Even though screwcap wines are becoming more prevelant, a corkscrew is still essential, and it is important to get a good one. Although there are plenty to choose from—such as the "waiter's friend" with a knife, the butterfly lever, and the basic wooden-handled ones—none surpasses the Screwpull, which very is easy to use.

- Buy some foil cutters at the same time as you buy a corkscrew; they remove the top of the capsule in one easy twist, saving irritation and broken nails.

- If you are planning to decant your wines, you will need a decanter and a funnel. These need not be grand or expensive; a simple carafe and a plastic funnel are adequate. Keep a flashlight or candle handy for spotting the approaching sediment when decanting wine (see p.166).

- Hot and cold sleeves—one for the microwave and one for the freezer—help bring a wine quickly to the correct serving temperature.

- Other useful accessories are a max./min. thermometer for your cellar or cupboard under the stairs; stopper corks, or Vacuvins and wine preservers; a champagne stopper; an ice bucket and a wine cooler. A small basket is useful for transporting wine from the cellar to the table.

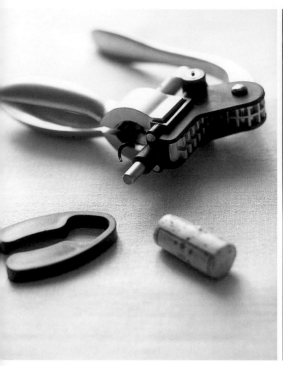

OPENING, DECANTING, & SERVING

Before serving a wine, decide whether it would benefit from being decanted first, and give it time to reach the appropriate temperature for drinking.

OPENING SPARKLING WINE

Remove the foil and wire, and hold the bottle at an angle with the bottom of the bottle in your strong hand and the cork in the other. Hold the cork firmly while slowly twisting the bottle, taking care not to shake it. Ease the cork out gently, covering it with the palm of your hand, while making sure you have a glass nearby in case the wine should froth out.

ICE BUCKETS AND COOLERS

If you are using an ice bucket, remember that plenty of water and a little ice will chill a bottle far more quickly and efficiently than plenty of ice and a little water. When using a wine cooler, bear in mind that it won't chill wine; it will simply keep the bottle at its starting temperature for a couple of hours.

DECANTING

Uncorking red wine hours before drinking doesn't make much difference—too little wine is exposed to the air to affect young wine, while the bouquet of old wine is apt to disappear. Far better to decant the wine, which rids an older wine of its sediment and gives a younger wine greater opportunity to "breathe." Even cheap wine is given a chance to show off. You don't have to use cut-glass decanters or silver funnels; a simple carafe—or even an empty, rinsed-out wine bottle—and a plastic funnel lined with filter-paper will do. If you are decanting without using filter-paper, pour the wine with a steady hand into the funnel, keeping an eye out for any sediment (a flashlight or candle is helpful here), and stop when the sediment reaches the neck.

SERVING TEMPERATURE

White wine should be cool enough to be refreshing, while red wine should be warm enough to exhibit its aroma and character. Ultimately, the temperature at which you serve a wine comes down to personal taste, so don't adhere too strictly to suggested levels—experience will tell you when you've got it right.

SUGGESTED TEMPERATURES FOR SERVING WHITE WINE

- 39–46°F for everyday sparkling wine and dessert wine, Riesling, and Vinho Verde.
- 46–52°F for champagne, top-quality sparkling wine and dessert wine, Gewurztraminer, Viognier, and rosé.
- 54–55°F for top-quality Alsace, Chardonnay, Sauvignon, and Sémillon.

SUGGESTED TEMPERATURES FOR SERVING RED WINE

- 50–55°F for lighter reds such as Beaujolais, red Loire, and Valpolicella.
- 57–61°F for young red burgundy and Rhône, older claret, Chianti, Rioja, and New World Pinot Noir.
- 61–64°F for older burgundy, Rioja and Barolo, young claret and Rhône, Zinfandel, and Shiraz.

SERVING TIPS

- When pouring wine, serve yourself before your guests, so you catch any stray bits of cork that might be floating around.
- The rule of thumb when serving several wines is: dry before sweet, white before red, and young before old.
- When pouring wine in front of your guests, have the label pointing uppermost so they can see what they are drinking.

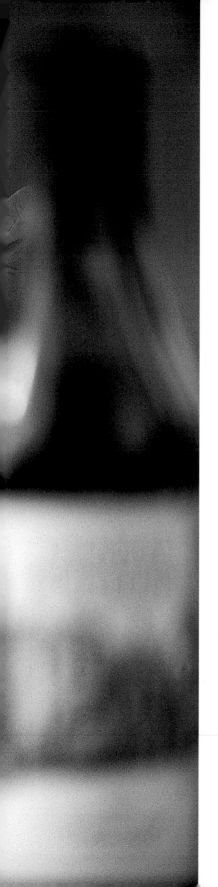

ORDERING IN A RESTAURANT

A meal out with family, friends, or co-workers is one of life's great pleasures, and in a perfect world the wine served would be as memorable as the food itself.

Indeed, a well-chosen bottle can make the most ordinary food seem special, just as a poorly-chosen one can mar the finest cooking. It is important to get it right. It is also important not to allow yourself to be bamboozled by either wine list or wine waiter (known as the sommelier).

In a top quality restaurant, the wine waiter is someone to lean on for advice; you should trust them, allowing them to be your guide, mentor, and friend. They will have probably tried most, if not all, the wines on the list and will have taken (and might even teach at) fully accredited wine courses. They will also be keen that you return to the restaurant and will give good advice. This can be less true of some establishments, whose staff don't know about wine and don't care if you come back or not. After all, they probably won't be there on your next visit. "Would you prefer the red or the white Chardonnay?" they ask, cheerfully.

More restaurants than you might imagine allow diners to bring their own bottles (BYO). Check this while booking. Restaurants mark their wines up by a huge amount (often absurdly and indecently), and taking your own special bottle and paying corkage is a cheaper and more pleasurable alternative.

Here are a few dos and don'ts to help you get through the ordeal of ordering wine in a restaurant:

- DO find out what everyone else around the table is going to eat before committing to a certain bottle. There is not much point going for that South African Pinotage you've got your eye on, if your companions are all having Dover sole.

- DO check that you are happy with the wine's temperature. If you want your white wine chilled, ask for an ice bucket and if you want the red a bit warmer ask for it to be put near a radiator. It's your money.

- DO confirm the name of the producer/shipper. Some very different quality wines have very similar names.

- DO check the vintage details of your bottle. Many restaurants substitute certain wines with subsequent vintages. This is all very well with a simple Muscadet, but you wouldn't want a 1990 claret replaced with one from the vastly inferior 1991 vintage.

- DO check that the bottle is brought to the table unopened, except perhaps house wine. Of course it never, ever happens that restaurants serve the topped up remnants of previous diners' wines. Oh, no...

- DO be wary of a list that has many cheap to mid-price wines but only one or two show-stoppers. These fancy wines may well have found their way here by a rather dubious route or are simply there to make the wine list look impressive. Either way, they almost certainly won't have been stored properly, and are probably stashed away under the patron's desk or next to the boiler.

- DO turn to the sommelier for advice, if the restaurant has one. There are far worse ways of choosing a wine than having it chosen for you by an expert. Tell him or her what your budget is, what you are eating, and what wines you have enjoyed in the past. You might get to meet your new favorite wine.

- DO ask about wines served by the glass. It is a great sadness that most restaurants only have a limited selection of such wines available—usually just their house wine or champagne, but other, more enlightened places have new-fangled machines that keep wines fresh for longer and are therefore in a position to offer several. It is still worth asking how long the wine has been opened and checking that what you get is what you ordered.

- DON'T be shy of sending a bottle back if you really think that something is wrong with it, you are not insulting the restaurateur by doing so. He didn't make the wine and it's not his fault (unless he has stored it really badly). And in any event, he will simply let his suppliers know and will get recompensed by them.

- DON'T think that you are able to send a wine back simply because you don't like it and are wishing that you had ordered the German Riesling rather than the California Chardonnay.

- DO be prepared to sample the wine when it arrives. Any restaurant worth its salt will invite you to take a sip of wine (except possibly house wine served from the carafe) before it is properly served. There is no need to get flustered, just take your time. Almost anything that could be wrong with a wine can be detected by looking at it (it should be clear and bright) and by smelling it (it will smell musty or like sherry if there is something amiss). It is hard to think of any good wine—other than perhaps white Rhône which can often smell like sherry—that doesn't flutter its eyelids at you.

- DON'T look impressed when the sommelier sniffs the cork after opening your bottle. This tells one absolutely nothing except that damp corks pulled straight from a bottle of wine smell like damp corks pulled straight from a bottle of wine.

- DON'T get embarrassed trying to pronounce a wine name that looks a bit tricky. Simply point to it on the list or identify it by its number if it has one.

- DON'T feel rushed. Take your time to get your bearings. The restaurant is unlikely to run out of stock before you have made your choice. Although the list might seem intimidating, it should give you all the facts that you need to make an informed decision.

TASTING WINE

You can leaf through any amount of books like this, but the only real way to learn about wine is to sample it yourself. What a wonderful subject to study, the research for which relies upon the regular opening of a bottle or two. The idea of tasting wine might seem intimidating, but in truth you do it every time you have a glass. Nothing to panic about.

You taste wine in three stages: by looking at the wine in the glass, sniffing it, and sipping it to see if you like it. As you become more advanced you may feel like making notes or discussing what you think. But remember, there is never a wrong answer. If you think a wine tastes like your mailman's boots while your neighbor detects warm hay on a summer's day, neither of you is right or wrong. It is how a wine tastes to you that is important.

HOW TO TASTE

It should go without saying that we use three of our five senses to evaluate wine. If you put a glass of wine to your ears it won't tell you much, unless you detect the effervescence of a sparkling wine. If you touch the wine you will learn only that it is wet, something which you might have gathered already. But look at it, smell it, and taste it and you will know everything there is to know:

• Fill about a quarter of your glass and look at the wine, preferably against a white background. It should be clear and bright, whatever its color.

- Holding the stem, twirl the glass around to release the wine's bouquet.

- Then take a deep sniff. It should smell clean and enticing and will almost certainly remind you of something else that has nothing to do with wine.

- Take a big sip, drawing air into the mouth as you do so. Swill it around and then, if you are pacing yourself at a tasting, spit into the nearest spittoon.

Tastes and smells might be the hardest of the senses to describe, but to be an effective wine taster you need to get into the habit of jotting down what tastes and smells mean to you, what they remind you of, and what they are like. There are dangers of sounding a bit airy-fairy and over the top, but it must be done.

Expressing touch is easy: things are soft, hard, wet, dry, and so on. You just have to hum a tune to illustrate a sound, and describing things you can see is a cinch. Smell and taste are not so easy. How do you put into words what smoke smells like? Or Eau de Cologne? How do you explain the difference in taste between roast lamb and roast beef? Or describe what scrambled eggs taste like, or baked beans? So it is that practiced wine tasters tend to equate wines with other tastes and smells, with similes rather than descriptions.

Bizarrely, very few wines, except those made from Muscat, actually taste or smell of grapes, and so it is important to identify a taste or smell that has nothing to do with the wine you are sampling which might help you recognize it again. Grass, nettles, cat's pee, gooseberries, black currant leaves are all aromas associated with Sauvignon Blanc, for example.

TERMINOLOGY
Wine words include: acidity, aroma, austere, baked, biscuity, bouquet, butter, closed, depth, dry, elegant, extract, finesse, finish, flabby, flinty, floral, jammy, legs, length, oaky, off-dry, oxidized, *pétillant*, restrained, minty, robust, sediment, short, spicy, steely, structure, sulphur, sweet, tannic, vanilla, vegetal, yeasty.

ARRANGING A TASTING FOR FRIENDS

- Don't have too many wines—four reds and four whites, perhaps, or eight of one color.

- Make sure white wines are adequately chilled, but not so cold as to subdue their aromas. Allow the reds to get to room temperature.

- Always taste the wines yourself first to make sure they are okay.

- Make sure that there are plenty of plain crackers, not just to soak up the alcohol, but to cleanse the palate between wines.

- The best tasting order is whites before reds, cheap before expensive, light before heavy, unoaked before oaked, dry before sweet, and fortified at the end.

You will need

- Pens and paper for taking notes.
- Some foil or paper with which to wrap the bottles and obscure the labels.
- Numbered cards to place in front of the bottles.
- A long table with a white tablecloth.
- Spittoons (boxes filled with sawdust, or empty pitchers work fine, but preferably not of clear glass as expectorated wine doesn't look too appetizing).
- Pitchers of water.
- Glasses (standard ISO glasses are best, or small, tear drop shaped ones with stems).
- Oh, and some bottles of wine. You should be able to get 16 good-size tasting samples per bottle.

TYPES OF TASTINGS AND THEMES

If you plan to taste wines with friends or colleagues, there are a number of ways to make this varied and interesting, although it is important to take into account the tasters' different levels of expertise. Even the uninitiated will find a wine tasting fascinating, and there is no need for it to be staid and formal.

- **Old World against New World.** This is always good value, comparing some Australian Shirazes with some Rhône Syrahs, or California Chardonnays with white burgundies.

- **Grape against grape.** It is only by tasting wines against each other that you will learn what you like and don't, and comparing two classic varieties, such as Cabernet Sauvignon against Merlot, is always interesting.

- **Blind tasting.** This is where the bottles are wrapped in foil or paper, and tasters have no information about the wines at all. This might seem intimidating, in that it gives you a chance to parade your ignorance to one and all, but in fact it is often liberating, in that you approach the bottles with no preconceptions and you will surprise yourself with how much you know.

- **Half-blind tasting.** You could tell your tasters that they are sampling wine from a particular country or region, but not what varieties or vintages. Or tell them the grape variety, but not the country or vintage.

- **The price test.** This is always good fun for wine lovers with different levels of expertise. Present 10 bottles, all obscured, and a sheet of paper with 10 prices on it. Ask your guests to match them. It is both easier and harder than you think.

- **Horizontal tasting.** A tasting of different wines from the same year.

- **Vertical tasting.** A tasting of the same wine from different vintages. This is best done with Old World wines, such as clarets or burgundies, where there are wider variations between vintages.

WINE FAULTS & CONTROVERSIES

WINE AND HEALTH

There are over 50 processing aids and additives permitted to be used in wines sold in the EU. Processing aids (which do not stay in the finished wine) include (vegetarians take note) gelatin (beef tissue), isinglass (ground fish tissue), casein (milk protein), egg albumen, bentonite, copper sulphate, caramel, calcium phytate, ammonium bisulphate, potassium ferrocyanide, and polyvinylpolypyrrolidone. Nevertheless, wine is a wonderfully natural product and medical evidence suggests, overwhelmingly, that it is good for us.

Research has identified the following health-giving properties in wine:

• Resveratrol, a natural chemical compound found especially in red wine, acts as an antibiotic agent and antioxidant and appears to play a role in preventing heart attacks, strokes, and cancer.

• Saponin, another antioxidant found in red wine, is thought to help in reducing levels of low-density lipoprotein (LDL) cholesterol.

• The "Whitehall Study" found that of 6,000 civil servants given psychometric tests, those who drank the equivalent of half a bottle of wine a day scored best of all, whilst teetotallers were twice as likely as occasional drinkers to achieve the lowest scores.

CORKS VS. SCREWCAPS

Screwcaps used to be synonymous with cheap wine; no longer. It is now generally accepted that at least one in every 20 bottles of wine is "corked" (see right), which is clearly not a problem with screwcaps. Occasionally, though, a wine might become contaminated before bottling, in which case the whole batch (rather than just one bottle) will be affected. It is fair to say that screwcaps cannot prevent bad wine if the wine was bad in the first place, but corks can ruin perfectly good wine.

There is heated debate about whether a wine ages as well in a screwcapped bottle as it does in one stoppered by a cork. It appears that screwcapped wines do develop in the bottle, but more slowly than those under cork (and the jury is out on long-term cellaring). The predominant aging reactions in the bottle are reductive, taking place in the absence of air, disproving the common notion that wines need to "breathe" through the cork. Most importantly, screwcaps benefit the impromptu drinker and those caught short without a corkscrew. Long live the revolution!

WINE FAULTS

- A "corked" wine is one that has been tainted by the cork—the most common cause of which is TCA (trichloroanisole)—a condition that taints the taste and smell of the wine and is usually heralded by a damp, musty odor. The term is often erroneously used to describe wine that is "off." It does not refer to any harmless fragments of cork that might remain in the glass or bottle.

- A maderized wine is one that is close to being oxidized, a condition often characterized by a deep orange hue and taste not dissimilar to sherry or madeira.

- An oxidized wine is one that has deteriorated owing to the wine's prolonged contact with too much air.

- Tartrates are small crystals of potassium bitartrate which sometimes appear in cask or bottle owing to the natural presence of tartaric acid. They are completely harmless.

- Bottle stink is the term given to the stale whiff—usually of bad eggs—that can hit the drinker as a bottle of wine is opened. It usually disappears within seconds and rarely means that anything is wrong with the wine.

WINE & FOOD

There is only one hard and fast rule to bear in mind when matching wine with food, and that is: Don't Be Afraid. Experiment!

Trial and error is the only way to find that perfect pairing where wine and food combine in harmony, each enhancing the other.

Generally speaking, the lighter the dish, the lighter the wine should be, and the heavier the dish, the heavier the wine. But try anything once, and if you get it wrong, stop. You will know better next time.

There are, of course, some classic combinations that are hard to beat, a chilled bottle of Muscadet Sur Lie with a plate of oysters, for example, a fine red burgundy with a dish of *boeuf bourgignon* (the beef is cooked in that wine after all), or an inky black Cahors with a steaming bowl of cassoulet, but such pairings are not etched in tablets of stone. Everyone's taste differs, and while you should always bear in mind the experience of those who have trodden this path before you, the only way to find out what you like is to try it for yourself.

Don't be scared of serving red wine with fish, for example; you will soon learn whether the pairing works to your taste or not. And a big raspberry to those who turn their noses up at you for committing social suicide. After all, what makes them better experts in your taste buds than you? Although it is true that most red wines are made to taste unpleasantly metallic by fish or seafood dishes, there are some combinations that work perfectly—Oregon Pinot Noir with salmon or tuna steak for example. Similarly, why restrict the sweet wine to accompanying desserts? A rich and luscious Sauternes, late harvest Australian Semillon, or Muscat de Beaumes-de-Venise goes just as well with pâté de foie gras at the start of a meal as it does with a strong blue cheese at the end.

In the Old World, wines have had centuries in which to evolve so that they match local cuisine perfectly and vice versa. It is no accident that the white wines of the Loire match seafood so well; that there is nothing better with Greek food than that acquired taste, Retsina; that Tokay Pinot Gris goes so well with a *choucroute Alsacienne*. The New World does not have this history of wine and food combinations, which perhaps allows it to be a bit more adventurous and daring.

The pairings listed below should be considered as no more than suggestions and ideas to set you on your way; wine was created to accompany food, and you will be surprised at some of the unlikely combinations that succeed. Be brave and enjoy.

APERITIFS Champagne or sparkling wine, if the occasion demands it, otherwise a well-chilled Fino or Manzanilla sherry will kick-start the most jaded of appetites. If you're bored with white wine, try a Beaujolais or red Sancerre straight from the refrigerator.

BEEF

BEEF POT PIE Something hearty like a Rhône, Italian Barolo, or Australian Shiraz.
BEEF STEWS AND CASSEROLES A robust red such as a Côte Rôtie or Hermitage from the Rhône, an Australian Shiraz, or a top-quality Rioja. Or try a big, oak-aged Chardonnay from Burgundy or Australia.
COLD ROAST BEEF (See Cold Cuts)
HAMBURGERS A young, fruity Chianti or Beaujolais or Spanish Tempranillo would work well, as would a Chilean Merlot or Cabernet Sauvignon. Or try a full-bodied white such as a Viognier or Australian oaked Semillon.
ROAST BEEF Any good red wine. Red might be the obvious choice, but a good quality Pinot Gris from Alsace will have the weight and the depth of flavor to make a very decent substitute.

SHEPHERD'S PIE A full-bodied Zinfandel or Côtes du Rhône.
STEAK A New World Cabernet Sauvignon is hard to beat.

BRUNCH Champagne or sparkling wine if your stomach can cope, a Bloody Mary if it can't. (And don't forget that the perfect Bloody Mary has a dash of Amontillado sherry added to it.)

CANAPES Sparkling wine, chilled Fino or Manzanilla sherry, or any light, dry white wine.

CASSOULET This dish is best accompanied by a French country wine such as Cahors, Madiran, or Corbières.

CHEESE

BLUE CHEESE (such as Stilton, St. Agur) An intensely sweet Sauternes or Beerenauslese can't be bettered. Vintage port is traditional, but why not try an Italian Barbera or Chilean Cabernet Sauvignon instead?
GOAT CHEESE White wine seems to work best: a bone-dry one, such as a classy Sauvignon Blanc from New Zealand or the Loire, or an intensely sweet one, such as a Sauternes or Vouvray.

GRILLED CHEESE Something young and full-bodied such as Chilean Merlot. Or a dry white Bordeaux or similar Rhône.
HARD CHEESES (such as Cheddar, Edam, Gloucester, Gouda) A middling quality claret or tawny port.
SOFT CHEESES (such as Camembert and Brie) Almost any red wine will do, but nothing fancy. An unoaked Chardonnay from Chablis, say, or the New World, often makes a better partner to such cheeses than a red wine would.
STRONG CHEESES (such as Roquefort, Munster) A late harvest Gewurztraminer from Alsace, or an Icewine from Canada—both served well-chilled—will make you wonder why you never tried such a pairing before. You could also try a rich madeira or Ruby port.

CHICKEN

CHICKEN IN CREAMY SAUCES Such dishes need something with a bit of character, like an Alsace Pinot Gris or a New Zealand Sauvignon Blanc.
CHICKEN LIVER PATE A dry white from Burgundy or Bordeaux, or even a Viognier.
CHICKEN POT PIE Try a

Chilean Cabernet Sauvignon or Merlot.

COLD CHICKEN For a red, choose something light, a Beaujolais perhaps, or red Loire, or any white wine with a bit of oomph to it, such as a white Rhône or a white Rioja.

COQ AU VIN Red burgundy is the obvious (and most authentic) choice, otherwise a good New World Pinot Noir.

ROAST CHICKEN Almost any red wine—a full-flavored white wine such as a New World Chardonnay or mature white burgundy will also hit the spot. (Save time and effort by French roasting the chicken: a large glass each of red wine and stock poured around the bird will keep the flesh deliciously moist, and provide you with a tasty gravy.)

CHILI CON CARNE Nothing fancy, a simple Chianti or Valpolicella is best, or an Argentinian Malbec.

CHINESE FOOD White wine for preference, such as anything from Alsace, a medium-dry German Riesling, or a Californian Chardonnay, but you could do worse than a New World Pinot or Beaujolais.

COLD CUTS A spread of ham, roast beef, and salami is best matched with a young fruity red from Bordeaux or the Rhône. Full-flavored and characterful white wines also work such as Alsace Pinot Gris, California Chardonnay, Australian Semillon/Chardonnay.

COOKIES Medium-dry madeira such as Bual or Rainwater or a tawny port. An Amontillado sherry or a medium-dry Vouvray.

DESSERTS
CAKE Oloroso or Cream sherry.
CHOCOLATE PUDDING The only wines that can really stand up to chocolate are the Black Muscats and Orange Muscats of California and Australia.
FRESH FRUIT Fruit can be tricky, so best stick to a sweet Coteaux du Layon or Vouvray.
FRUIT TARTS German or Austrian Beerenauslese, or a late harvest Alsace Gewurztraminer.
ICE CREAM AND SORBETS Take a break from the wine here, and come back to it afterwards.
STRAWBERRIES AND CREAM A sweet Vouvray or a sweet sparkler like Asti Spumante.

DUCK
BROILED DUCK BREASTS Zinfandel or an oaky Rioja.
ROAST DUCK A full-bodied red such as Barolo, Hermitage, Châteauneuf-du-Pape, or Australian Shiraz. If you prefer a white wine an aromatic Viognier, top-quality Chablis, or Alsace is needed.

EGG DISHES Eggs aren't the ideal partners for wine, but a plate of scrambled eggs and smoked salmon always seems to demand champagne or top-quality sparkling wine.

FISH
FISH AND CHIPS Why not champagne? Otherwise a crisp white such as Chablis, or even, given that this is such a traditional English dish, a dry English wine.
FISH IN CREAMY SAUCES Such dishes are well-partnered by Riesling—from Australia, Alsace or Germany.
BOUILLABAISSE Any dry wine from the Loire—a Pouilly Fumé or Sancerre if you are in funds, a Muscadet or Sauvignon de Touraine if you are not.
FISH PATE An aromatic Viognier or an Alsace Riesling would be perfect.
FISH PIE Try a Sauvignon Blanc from New Zealand or Chile, or a new wave Spanish Albariño.
FRITTO MISTO A light, dry Italian such as Verdicchio, Orvieto, or Frascati.
GRAVADLAX Chablis, New World Chardonnay, or Viognier.

GRILLED SALMON Chablis, white burgundy, or New World Chardonnay. It may surprise you, but some fish dishes do go well with red wine, and an Oregon Pinot Noir would be perfect here.
GRILLED SHRIMP Any dry white wine will do.
GRILLED SOLE OR PLAICE Such a simple dish will allow any top-quality wine to show off, such as the best white burgundy or Chablis you can lay your hands on.
GRILLED TROUT Try an English wine.
GRILLED TURBOT AND TUNA A white Rhône or an Australian Riesling.
RED MULLET A well-chilled red Loire or a classy dry rosé.
SMOKED EEL, MACKEREL, AND SALMON Australian Semillon or Alsace Gewurztraminer.
SMOKED HADDOCK OR COD White Rhône or full-bodied Chardonnay.
TUNA STEAKS Try a top-class Beaujolais or even a New World Pinot Noir.

FOIE GRAS Top quality sweet wine such as Sauternes, Alsace Vendange Tardive, or Canadian Icewine. Otherwise a dry Viognier.

GAME Meats such as grouse, hare, partridge, pheasant,

pigeon, rabbit, venison, or wild boar, whether roasted or casseroled need hefty, big-boned wines such as California Cabernet Sauvignon, Barolo, a fine Rhône, or Rioja.
GOOSE This deserves a claret or a red burgundy. For a white wine, something big and highly-flavored is needed, such as an Alsace Pinot Gris or an Hermitage Blanc. You might even consider an off-dry Riesling such as a German Spätlese.

GREEK FOOD Retsina is the obvious choice for the taramasalata and calamari, but as it is something of an acquired taste you might prefer a Muscadet or an Italian Chardonnay. Stick to white for the appetizers and then a rustic red from Greece, southern France, Lebanon, or north Africa for the moussaka and lamb kabobs.

GRILLED MEAT A red with a bit of zing is required here, such as a New World Zinfandel, Pinotage, or Australian Shiraz, or perhaps a meaty Rhône or southern French country wine.

HAM (See Cold Cuts)

INDIAN Beer is the obvious choice, but failing that, try a

well-chilled light red such as Beaujolais, or an ice-cold medium-dry Vouvray, or an off-dry Orvieto.

LAMB
LAMB CHOPS OR CUTLETS Any flavorsome red will do, an Australian Cabernet-Shiraz blend perhaps, a Rioja Gran Reserva, or a classy Merlot-based claret.
ROAST LAMB This classic dish deserves a fine red Bordeaux or New World Cabernet Sauvignon. Something full-flavored but dry is needed if you are eschewing red wine, like an Hermitage Blanc.
SHEPHERD'S PIE A Crozes-Hermitage, Côtes du Rhône, or California Zinfandel work well.

LIVER
CALFS' LIVER AND ONIONS The Viennese and Venetians may fight over who invented this dish, but Italian reds such as Bardolino, Valpolicella, or Chianti are the best accompaniments.

MEXICAN FOOD A spicy Zinfandel is needed here, or a peppery Rhône such as St. Joseph or Cornas. For whites, try Sauvignon Blancs from Chile, California, or New Zealand.

MOUSSAKA (See Greek Food)

NORTH AFRICAN FOOD A Moroccan or Algerian red wine if you can find one, or the excellent Château Musar from the Lebanon. For whites, stick to full-bodied wines from the Rhône or the New World.

NUTS Madeira or tawny port.

OLIVES Dry sherry works best of all.

ONION TART (See Quiche)

PASTA
WITH BOLOGNESE SAUCE Any Italian red, but ideally a Chianti Classico.
WITH NEAPOLITAN SAUCE Ditto, but with Barbera as the first choice.
WITH SEAFOOD SAUCE Almost any white wine from Italy, such as Orvieto, Frascati, Soave, or Verdicchio.

WITH PESTO SAUCE The same as for pasta with seafood sauce, although simple unoaked Chardonnay works well too.

PATES AND TERRINES It depends on what they are made from, but any smooth, soft red should do.

PICNICS If taking red wine to a picnic, open it beforehand and recork it, even decant it and rebottle it. (It means that you can taste it beforehand to check that it is okay and clear of sediment, and that you don't have to worry about forgetting the corkscrew. It also allows instant access to alcohol, ensuring that that special moment is not lost...) As for whites, a well-chilled French country wine such as a Côtes de Gascogne if there are lots of you, but treat yourselves to vintage champagne if there are only the two of you.

PIZZA For authenticity, you really should have an Italian red, but in truth almost anything red and uncomplicated will do, unless it is smothered in anchovies.

PORK
LOIN OF PORK A good Pinot Noir won't let you down, but if you want white, an Australian Semillon also works well.

ROAST PORK Any good red wine goes well with roast pork, but, just for the fun of it, why not try one from Portugal or New Zealand? Any full-bodied white wine will do, too.

PROSCIUTTO WITH MELON Try an Italian white such as Orvieto, Lugana, Frascati, or Verdicchio.

QUICHE AND ONION TART

Something light like an Alsace or Oregon Pinot Noir or perhaps a Beaujolais, or Australian Riesling, or, classically, a white Alsace.

RISOTTO Any red from Italy or the Loire, or an Italian Pinot Grigio.

SALADS It depends on the dressing and on what is in the salad, but a light red should certainly do the trick, or a dry and light white, such as a Muscadet or South American Sauvignon Blanc.

SEAFOOD

CAVIAR If you are eating caviar it probably means that someone else is paying, so insist on champagne.

COLD LOBSTER This really demands a first rate white burgundy or New World equivalent.

DRESSED CRAB Dry German Riesling or white Rhône.

LOBSTER THERMIDOR This dish gives you the chance to dig out an old white burgundy, top quality New World Chardonnay or Hermitage Blanc.

SAUTEED SCALLOPS Dry German or Australian Riesling or New Zealand Sauvignon Blanc.

OYSTERS Chablis, Sancerre, Pouilly Fumé or Black Velvet (champagne and draught Guinness, half and half, in a pint tankard).

MOULES ET FRITES Muscadet, Italian Pinot Grigio or, best of all, unfiltered Belgian wheat beer.

SHEPHERD'S PIE (See Lamb)

SOUP A Sercial madeira makes a change from the traditional dry sherry.

SUSHI AND SASHIMI Sake (served hot) or full-flavored New World Chardonnay.

TAPAS Nothing goes better with tapas than Manzanilla sherry.

THAI Beaujolais or red Loire, or, best of all, a spicy New World or Alsace Gewurztraminer.

TURKEY

ROAST TURKEY This most boring of dishes needs a decent red to take your mind off it.

COLD TURKEY So does this.

VEAL

ROAST VEAL Something soft and mature is best, like an old claret, red burgundy, or Rioja. Otherwise a big, oak-aged Chardonnay from Burgundy or Australia.

VEAL IN CREAM SAUCE Pouilly-Fumé or Sancerre or even Alsace Riesling.

VEAL IN MARSALA SAUCE A full-bodied Alsace Pinot Gris works well here, or an Australian Verdelho.

VEGETABLES

ROAST VEGETABLES An oaky Chardonnay from Australia or California is ideal.

WINE WORDS

Acidity A feature of wine—natural acids give wine character and structure and help it age.

Aerate Bring a wine into contact with air to accelerate its development.

Alcohol Sugar in ripe grapes turns into alcohol to produce wine.

Aroma The smell of a wine.

Balance A wine's harmonious combination of acids, tannins, alcohol, fruit, and flavor.

Bereich (German) Wine-producing district.

Bianco (Italian) White.

Blanc (French) White.

Blanc de blancs (French) White wine made only from white grapes.

Blanc de noirs (French) White wine made only from black (red) grapes.

Blanco (Spanish) White.

Blend Mixture of more than one grape variety.

Blind tasting Wine tasting at which labels and shapes of bottles are concealed from tasters.

Bodega (Spanish) Winery.

Body Weight and structure of a wine.

Botrytis cinerea Fungus that shrivels and rots white grapes, concentrating their flavors and sugars; creates dessert wines high in alcohol and richness of flavor. Also known as noble rot, pourriture noble, and edelfäule.

Bouquet Complex scent of a wine that develops as it matures.

Cantina (Italian) Winery or cellar.

Cepa (Spanish) Vine variety.

Cépage (French) Vine variety.

Chai (French) Place for storing wine.

Chambrer (French) Allow a wine gradually to reach room temperature before drinking it.

Château (French) Wine-growing property—used chiefly in Bordeaux.

Claret Red wine of Bordeaux.

Clos (French) Enclosed vineyard.

Colheita (Portuguese) Vintage; also used to denote a single vintage port.

Complex (said of a wine) Marked by a variety of flavors.

Concentrated (said of a wine) Marked by depth, richness, and fruitiness.

Core Color of wine in the center of a glass.

Corkage Charge per bottle levied on customers in restaurants who bring in their own wine to drink.

Corked Condition, revealed by a musty odor, where a wine has been contaminated by a faulty cork.

Cosecha (Spanish) Vintage.

Côte (French) Hillside of vineyards.

Crémant (French) Semi-sparkling.

Cru (French) Growth or vineyard.

Cru Classé (French) Classed Growth, especially 61 red wines of the Médoc (and one from the Graves) in Bordeaux graded into five categories according to price in 1855. Similar classifications followed elsewhere in Bordeaux for Graves red wines in 1953 and for St. Emilion in 1954 (revised 1969 and 1985).

Cuvée (French) Blended wine or special selection.

Demi-sec (French) Semi-sweet.

Dolce (Italian) Sweet.

Domaine (French) Property or estate.

Doux (French) Sweet.

Dulce (Spanish) Sweet.

Extract Concentration of fruit in a wine.

Fermentation Transformation of grape juice into wine, whereby yeasts—naturally present in grapes and occasionally added in cultured form—convert sugars into alcohol.

Finesse Complexity and subtlety in a wine.

Flavor Aroma and taste of a wine, compared to fruits, spices and so on.

Fortified wine Wine—such as port, sherry, or madeira—to which alcohol has been added either to stop it from fermenting before all its sugars turn to alcohol or simply to strengthen it.

Frizzante (Italian) Semi-sparkling.

Full-bodied (said of wine) Marked by a high level of fruit concentration and alcohol.

Grand cru (French) Top-quality wines from Alsace, Bordeaux, Burgundy, and Champagne.

Halbtrocken (German) Medium dry.

Horizontal tasting Tasting of several different wines all from the same vintage.

Integrated (said of wine) Where tannins in a wine are harmonious with the other components of the wine.

Jahrgang (German) Vintage.

Landwein (German) A level of quality wine just above simple table wine, equivalent to the French vin de pays.

Late harvest (said of grapes) Very ripe grapes that have been picked late when their sweetness is most concentrated.

Legs Thickness left on the inside of the glass by some wines.

Length (said of wine) How long the taste of a wine lasts after it has been swallowed or spat out.

Meritage Term coined in 1988 for California wines blended from the classic red varieties of Bordeaux.

Méthode champenoise Method by which champagnes and top-quality sparkling wines are made; involves a secondary fermentation in bottle.

Moelleux (French) Sweet.

Mousse (French) Effervescence in a glass of

sparkling wine as it is poured.

Mousseux (French) Sparkling.

Négociant (French) Wine merchant, shipper, or grower who buys wine or grapes in bulk from several sources before vinifying and/or bottling the wine himself.

Noble rot Botrytis cinera fungus, which attacks grape skins and results in super-concentration.

Non-vintage (NV) A wine that is a blend of more than one vintage, notably champagne.

Nose The qualities of a wine that create the sensation experienced by smelling it. This is not just a matter of the wine's scent; the nose also conveys information about the wine's wellbeing.

Oak Wine aged in oak barrels can be identified by whiffs of vanilla or cedarwood.

Oxidized (said of wine) Wine that has deteriorated as a result of its overexposure to air.

Palate Taste of a wine in the mouth.

Perlant (French) Very faintly sparkling.

Perlwein (German) A type of low-grade semi-sparkling wine.

Pétillant (French) Slightly sparkling.

Phylloxera Aphidlike insect that attacks the roots of grapevines with disastrous results.

Punt Indentation at the bottom of a bottle which catches any sediment and strengthens the bottle.

Quinta (Portuguese) Wine-growing estate.

Récolte (French) Crop or vintage.

Rich (said of wine) With a good concentration of ripe fruit.

Rosso (Italian) Red.

Rouge (French) Red.

Sec (French) Dry.

Secco (Italian) Dry.

Seco (Spanish/Portuguese) Dry.

Sediment Deposit that forms after a wine has spent a long time in a bottle.

Sekt (German) Sparkling wine.

Smooth (said of wine) With good fruit levels and soft integrated tannins.

Soft (said of wine) Rounded, fruity, low in tannin.

Sparkling (said of wine) Produced to have bubbles.

Spritzer Refreshing drink made from white wine and club soda or sparkling spring water, and often served with ice.

Spumante (Italian) Sparkling.

Sulphur Pungent smell given off by wine that can be dispersed by swirling the glass.

Sur lie (said of wine) Aged on its lees or sediment before bottling—resulting in a greater depth of flavor.

Sweetness A quality of wine created by unfermented sugar deriving from the ripeness of the grapes.

Tannin Austere acid found in some red wines deriving from grape skins and stalks combined with the oak barrels in which the wine has been aged; it is a necessary preservative.

Tafelwien (German) Table wine.

Tartrates Harmless crystals that can be found in both red and white wines.

Tastevin A small silver tasting dish, most commonly used in Burgundy.

Tears Thickness left on the inside of the glass by some wines.

Terroir (French) Meaning literally "soil" or "earth," terroir encompasses climate, drainage, position and anything else that distinguishes the taste of a wine from that of its immediate neighbours which have been grown and produced in the same way.

Texture What a wine feels like in the mouth; it is often compared to the feel of fabrics.

Tinto (Spanish/Portuguese) Red.

Trocken (German) Dry.

Ullage Amount of air in a bottle or barrel between the top of the wine and the base of the cork or bung.

Varietal Wine named after the grape (or the major constituent grape) from which it is made.

Variety Breed of grape.

Vendange (French) Harvest or vintage.

Vendange tardive (French) Late harvest.

Vendemmia (Italian) Harvest or vintage.

Vendimia (Spanish) Harvest or vintage.

Vertical tasting Tasting of several wines from the same property that are all from different vintages.

Vigneron (French) Wine grower.

Vin de pays (French) Country wine of a level higher than table wine.

Vin de table (French) Table wine.

Vin doux naturel (VDN) (French) Fortified wine that has been sweetened and strengthened by the addition of alcohol, either before or after fermentation.

Vin ordinaire (French) Basic wine not subject to any regulations.

Vinification Winemaking.

Vino da tavola (Italian) Table wine.

Vino de mesa (Spanish) Table wine.

Vintage Year of a grape harvest and the wine made from the grapes of that harvest.

Viscosity Thickness in a wine with a great density of fruit extract and alcohol—indicated by "tears" or "legs" on the side of the glass.

Viticulture Cultivation of grapes.

Weight Body and/or strength of a wine.

Winery Winemaking establishment.

USEFUL WEBSITES

BEST WINE MERCHANTS:
www.bbr.com
www.oddbins.com
www.wine.com
www.majestic.com
www.uvine.com

BEST WINE TOURS:
www.winetours.co.uk: Arblaster & Clarke Wine Tours, the leading wine tour operator's site. They cater for individual or group tours to most of the major wine growing regions of the world.
www.winetrails.co.uk: Group or individual tours either walking or cycling. A wonderful site to browse.
www.gourmet-touring.com: A small company specialising in classic car tours around the vineyards of Bordeaux.

BEST WINE EDUCATORS:
www.wset.co.uk
www.wineeducators.com
www.wineeducation.org
www.wine.gurus.com

BEST WINE MAGAZINES:
www.decanter.com: Companion site to the best-selling consumer wine magazine *Decanter* with an interesting "Learning Route" area and good wine news and features.
www.wine-pages.com: An e-zine, daily updated, with a wealth of news information as well as quizzes and tasting notes.
www.wineint.com: Companion to *Wine International* magazine. Includes information on the International Wine Challenge.
www.harpers-wine.com: On-line

Harpers, the wine trade's magazine. It has an extensive library of past features.
www.winespectator.com: The online version of the wine magazine from the US.

BEST WINE INFORMATION:
www.jancisrobinson.com: As one might expect from one of the UK's most respected wine writers, Jancis Robinson's site is an invaluable mine of information, especially the "subscription-only" area—the Purple Pages.
www.erobertparker.com: The site of the world's most influential wine critic. An annual subscription of $99 will give you access to the constantly updated database of over 70,000 tasting notes.

BEST WINE LINKS:
www.vine2wine.com
www.wine-searcher.com
Both intermediary sites that offer reviews of hundreds of wine-related sites.

BEST OTHER:
www.foodandwinematching.co.uk: Can't think what to serve with coq au vin? This will tell you.
www.awri.com.au: the Australian Wine Research Institute's website with a great section on wine and health.

BUSINESS CREDITS

Allied Domecq Wines (NZ) Ltd
171 Pilkington Rd
Auckland 1130
New Zealand
t. +64 9 5708400
www.adwnz.com
Page 127ar

Azienda Agricola Maculan
Producer Fausto Maculan
Via Castelletto, 3
36042 Breganze, VI
Italy
t. +39 0445 873733
f. +39 0445 300149
www.maculan.net
info@maculan.net

Pages 27a & r, 79bc, 142bl, 148l & c

Berry Brothers & Rudd Ltd
63 Palmal
London SW1Y 5HZ
UK
t. +44 20 7396 9666
f. +44 20 7396 9677
www.bbr.com
Pages 144–145l & 154

Bouchard Père et Fils
Château de Beaune
21200 Beaune
France
t. +33 3 80 24 80 24
www.bouchard-pereetfils.com

bpf@bouchard-pereetfils.com
Pages 63bl & bc, 146 & 147a, 192

Castello D'Abola
Via Pian d'Albola, 31
53017 Radda in Chianti, SI
Italy
t +39 0577 738019
f. +39 0577 738793
www.albola.it or www.albola.com
info@albola.it
Page 35

Chateau Montelena Winery
1429 Tubbs Lane
Calistoga, CA 94515
USA

t. +1 707 942 5105
www.montelena.com
Pages 24br, 57, 105br, 172, 173l & r

Col d'Orcia
Sant' Angelo in Colle
53020 Montalcino, SI
Italy
t. +39 0577 808911
f. +39 0577 844018
www.coldorcia.it
info@coldorcia.it
Page 60br

Craggy Range Vineyards
253 Waimarama Road
PO Box 8749

Havelock North
Hawkes Bay
New Zealand
t. +64 (0) 6 873 7126
www.craggyrange.com
Pages 127al & bl, 129l & br

Jordan Vineyard & Winery
1474 Alexander Valley Road
Healdsburg, CA 95448–9003
USA
t. +1 800 654 1213
www.JordanWinery.com
Pages 2–3, 14r, 105ac & bl,
108–109a & 108br, 171

M. Chapoutier
18 ave du Dr Paul Durand
26600 Tain l'Hermitage
France
t. +33 4 75 08 28 65
www.chapoutier.com
chapoutier@chapoutier.com
Pages 12a, 20bl, 22, 63al & ar, 68,
136l & r, 152, 156br & 157r

Maison Trimbach
15 route de Bergheim
68150 Ribeauvillé
France
t. +33 03 89 73 60 30
f. +33 03 89 73 89 04
www.maison-trimbach.fr
contact@maison-trimbach.fr
Pages 16b, 74l, 142br

New Zealand Winegrowers
New Zealand House
80 Haymarket
London SW1Y 4TE
UK
t. +44 207 973 8079
f. +44 207 973 0362

www.nzwine.com
Pages 127al & bl, 127ar, 127br,
129l & br

Nobilo Wine Group Ltd
45 Station Road, Huapai
PO Box 471, Kumeu
Auckland
New Zealand
t: +64 (09) 412 6666
www.nobilo.co.nz
Page 127br

Nyetimber Vineyard
Gay Street
West Chiltington
West Sussex
RH20 2HH
t. +44 (0)1798 813989
www.nyetimber-vineyard.com
info@nyetimber-vineyard.com
Pages 134al, ar & br

Riedel Crystal
t. +44 1782 646 105
www.riedel.com
Pages 162–163

Ridge Vineyards
www.ridgewine.com
wine@ridgewine.com
Pages 25 & 106
(two locations)
17100 Monte Bello Road
Cupertino, CA 95014
USA
Tasting: Sat & Sun 11–4pm, closed
holidays
t. +1 408 867 3233
f. +1 408 868 1350

650 Lytton Springs Road
Healdsburg, CA 95448
USA
Tasting: Daily 11–4pm, closed
holidays
t. +1 707 433 7721
f. +1 707 433 7751

Ruinart
4 Rue des Crayéres
51 100 Reims
France
t. +33 3 26 77 51 51
f. +33 3 26 82 88 43
www.ruinart.com
Pages 19a & bc–br, 20br, 63br, 158b

Scrimaglio Winery
Mario Scrimaglio
Pier Giorgio Scrimaglio
Francesco Scrimaglio
Strada Alessandria N.67
14049 Nizza Monferrato, AT
Italy
t. +39 0141 721385
f. +39 0141 726500
www.scrimaglio.it
info@scrimaglio.it
Pages 14c, 16a, 79bl, 80, 134bc,
142ar, 148r, 158a, 160r, 173c

Spiral Cellars (UK) Ltd
t. +44 20 8834 7371
www.spiralcellars.com
Pages 156–157a, 160l

Symington Family Estates
Travessa Barão de Forrester
4431–702 Vila Nova de Gaia
Portugal
t. +351 22 377 6300
www.symington.com
Pages 97–99, 138

Viña Concha y Toro S.A.
Pirque Casona, Don Melchor Casona
& Puente Alto Cellar
Avenida Nueva Tajamar 481
Torre Norte, Piso 15
Las Condes, Santiago
Chile
t. +56 2 476 5000
f. +56 2 476 5186
www.conchaytoro.com
enquiries@conchaytoro.cl
Pages 13b, 113ar, 116r–117, 168,
170, 176–177a

Viña Errázuriz S.A.
Avenida Nueva Tajamar 481
Oficina 503 Torre Sur
Las Condes, Santiago
Chile
t. +56 2 339 9100
f. +56 2 203 6690
www.errazuriz.cl
Pages 113bl, 114–115, 147b

**Weinbau-Domäne Schloss
Johannisberg**
www.schloss-johannisberg.com
Page 101

William Fèvre
21 Avenue D'Oberwesel
89800 Chablis
France
t. +33 3 86 98 98 98
www.williamfevre.com
france@williamfevre.com
Pages 4, 63ac, 67, 160c

Wines of South Africa
www.wosa.co.za
Pages 131a & bl, 132

PICTURE CREDITS

Photography by Alan Williams unless otherwise stated.
Key: **ph**= photographer, **a**=above, **b**=below, **r**=right, **l**=left, **c**=center.

2–3 Jordan Vineyard & Winery of Sonoma County, California; **4** William Fèvre, Grands Vin de Chablis, France; **12a** Maison M. Chapoutier, Châteauneuf-du-Pape, France; **13b** Viña Concha y Toro, Maipo Valley, Chile; **14c** Scrimaglio Winery, Italy; **14r** Jordan Vineyard & Winery of Sonoma County, California; **16a** Scrimaglio Winery, Italy; **16b** Maison Trimbach in Ribeauvillé, Alsace, France; **19a & bc–br** Champagne Ruinart, Reims, France—plus ancienne maison de champagne; **19bl ph** Peter Cassidy; **20bl** Maison M. Chapoutier, Tain l'Hermitage & Châteauneuf-du-Pape, France; **20br** Champagne Ruinart, Reims, France—plus ancienne maison de champagne; **22** Maison M. Chapoutier, Châteauneuf-du-Pape, France; **24ar ph** Peter Cassidy; **24br** Chateau Montelena Winery, Napa Valley, California; **25** Monte Bello, Ridge Vineyards, Santa Cruz Mountains, California; **27a & r** Azienda Agricola Maculan, Breganze; **35** Castello D'Abola, Radda in Chianti, Tuscany, Italy; **53 ph** Francesca Yorke; **57** Chateau Montelena Winery, Napa Valley, California; **60br** Tenuta Col d'Orcia, Montalcino; **63al & ar** Maison M. Chapoutier, Tain l'Hermitage, France; **63ac** William Fèvre, Grands Vin de Chablis, France; **63bl & bc** Bouchard Père et Fils, Grands Vin de Bourgogne, France; **63br** Champagne Ruinart, Reims, France—plus ancienne maison de champagne; **67** William Fèvre, Grands Vin de Chablis, France; **68** Maison M. Chapoutier, Tain l'Hermitage & Châteauneuf-du-Pape, France; **74l** Maison Trimbach in Ribeauvillé, Alsace, France; **75 ph** David Munns; **79bl** Scrimaglio Winery, Italy; **79bc** Azienda Agricola Maculan, Breganze; **80** Scrimaglio Winery, Italy; **97** © courtesy of Symington Family Estates, Portugal / **al & ac ph** Miguel Potes, **ar & b ph** Rui Cuhna; **98–99** © courtesy of Symington Family Estates, Portugal / **ph** Rui Cuhna; **101** © courtesy of Weinbau-Domäne Schloss Johannisberg / **al, ar & bl ph** Kurt Mayer, **bc ph** Martin Joppen; **102 & 105al ph** Francesca Yorke; **105ac & bl** Jordan Vineyard & Winery of Sonoma County, California; **105br** Chateau Montelena Winery, Napa Valley, California; **106** Monte Bello, Ridge Vineyards, Santa Cruz Mountains, California; **108l ph** Peter Cassidy; **108–109a & 108br** Jordan Vineyard & Winery of Sonoma County, California; **113ar** Viña Concha y Toro, Casablanca Valley, Chile; **113bl** Viña Errázuriz, Aconcagua Valley, Chile; **114–115** Viña Errázuriz, Don Maximiano Estate, Aconcagua Valley, Chile; **116r–117** Viña Concha y Toro, Maipo Valley, Chile; **121bl ph** Francesca Yorke; **127al & bl** © images supplied to New Zealand Winegrowers courtesy of Craggy Range Vineyards; **127ac ph** Francesca Yorke; **127ar** © images supplied to New Zealand Winegrowers courtesy of Allied Domecq Wines (NZ) Ltd; **127br** © images supplied to New Zealand Winegrowers courtesy of Nobilo Wine Group Ltd; **129l & br** © images supplied to New Zealand Winegrowers courtesy of Craggy Range Vineyards; **131a & bl** © courtesy of Wines of South Africa / **131al ph** Sven Lennert, **131ac, ar & bl ph** Aline Balayer; **132** © courtesy of Wines of South Africa / **ph** Aline Balayer; **134al, ar & br** © courtesy of Nyetimber Vineyard, England; **134bc** Scrimaglio Winery, Italy; **136l & r** Maison M. Chapoutier, Tain l'Hermitage, France; **138** © courtesy of Symington Family Estates, Portugal / **ph** Rui Cuhna; **142ar** Scrimaglio Winery, Italy; **142bl** Azienda Agricola Maculan, Breganze; **142br** Maison Trimbach in Ribeauvillé, Alsace, France; **144–145l** Berry Brothers & Rudd Ltd, London; **146 & 147a** Bouchard Père et Fils, Grands Vin de Bourgogne, France; **147b** Viña Errázuriz, Chile; **148l & c** Azienda Agricola Maculan, Breganze; **148r** Scrimaglio Winery, Italy; **149 ph** Francesca Yorke; **152** Maison M. Chapoutier, Châteauneuf-du-Pape, France; **154** Berry Brothers & Rudd Ltd, London; **156–157a** ph Dan Duchars / A wine cellar in a house in Surrey designed by Spiral Cellars Ltd; **156br & 157r** Maison M. Chapoutier, Tain l'Hermitage & Châteauneuf-du-Pape, France; **158a** Scrimaglio Winery, Italy; **158b** Champagne Ruinart, Reims, France—plus ancienne maison de champagne; **160l ph** Dan Duchars / A wine cellar in a house in Surrey designed by Spiral Cellars Ltd; **160c** William Fèvre, Grands Vin de Chablis, France; **160r** Scrimaglio Winery, Italy; **164 & 166r ph** Francesca Yorke; **168** Chateau Montelena Winery, Napa Valley, California; **170** Viña Concha y Toro, Chile; **171** Jordan Vineyard & Winery of Sonoma County, California; **172, 173l & r** Chateau Montelena Winery, Napa Valley, California; **173c** Scrimaglio Winery, Italy; **174–175 ph** Francesca Yorke; **176–177a** Viña Concha y Toro, Maipo Valley, Chile; **179 ph** James Merrell; **180a ph** Nicky Dowey; **180b & 182 ph** James Merrell; **183 ph** Peter Cassidy; **192** Bouchard Père et Fils, Grands Vin de Bourgogne, France.

INDEX

Abruzzo, 85
Aconcagua Valley, 117
Adelaide Hills, 124
aging, 16
Aglianico del Vulture, 86
Albariño, 146
Alentejo, 99
Algarve, 99
Algeria, 40
Alicante, 40, 95
Aligoté, 56
Aloxe-Corton, 67, 148
Alsace, 28, 51, 53, 54,
    55, 75, 137, 147, 150,
    153
Alto Adige, 26, 51, 53,
    54, 57, 82, 83, 146
Amarone, 149
Amontillado, 140
Anjou, 39, 52
aperitifs, 180
Apulia, 86
Argentina, 26, 32, 34, 35,
    37, 39, 40, 51,
    118–19, 149
aspect, vineyards, 13
Asti, 55, 81, 145
auctions, buying wine, 155
Aude, 40, 41
Auslese, 51, 151
Australia, 120–5
    Cabernet Sauvignon, 25
    Chardonnay, 45
    Chenin Blanc, 52
    Colombard, 58
    fortified wines, 141
    Gewurztraminer, 53
    Grenache, 33
    Marsanne, 59
    Merlot, 26
    Mourvèdre, 40
    Muscat, 55
    Pinot Noir, 28
    Riesling, 51
    Sémillon, 48
    Shiraz, 149
    sparkling wines, 145
    sweet wines, 137

Syrah (Shiraz), 31
Austria, 51, 53, 54, 55,
    135, 137, 147

Baden, 54, 103
Bairrada, 98
Bandol, 40, 77, 149
Banyuls, 33, 77, 149
Barbaresco, 37, 81, 149,
    150, 159
Barbera, 37, 81
Bardolino, 82, 147
Barolo, 37, 81, 149, 150,
    159
Barossa Valley, 31, 33,
    124
barrels, 14, 16, 45
Barsac, 47, 48, 65, 137,
    147
Basilicata, 86
Beaujolais, 23, 39, 67,
    147, 150
Beaune, 28, 67, 148
Beerenauslese, 51, 151
Bergerac, 77
Bierzo, 92
Blanquette de Limoux, 52,
    77, 145
blended wines, 15, 16
Bordeaux, 23, 25, 32, 39,
    41, 47, 48, 64–5, 117,
    147, 148
Bordeaux-style bottles,
    150
botrytis, 52, 135, 137
bottle stink, 177
bottles, 150
Bourg and Blaye, 26, 39,
    148
Bourgueil, 32, 73, 147
Bourgogne Passe-Tout-
    Grains, 28, 39
Brunello di Montalcino,
    35, 85
Bucelas, 99
Bull's Blood, 135
Burgundy, 15, 28, 39, 45,
    56, 66–7, 146, 148,
    153
Burgundy-style bottles,
    150

buying wine, 154–9

Cabernet Franc, 32, 147
Cabernet Sauvignon, 12,
    23, 25, 148, 149, 150,
    158
Cahors, 77, 149
Calabria, 86
California, 107–9
    Cabernet Franc, 32
    Cabernet Sauvignon, 25
    Carignan, 40
    Chardonnay, 45
    Chenin Blanc, 52
    Colombard, 58
    fortified wines, 141
    Gewurztraminer, 53
    Grenache, 33
    Malbec, 39
    Marsanne, 59
    Merlot, 26
    Mourvèdre, 40
    Muscat, 55
    Pinot Blanc, 54
    Pinot Gris, 54
    Pinot Noir, 28
    Riesling, 51
    Sauvignon Blanc, 47
    Silvaner, 55
    sparkling wines, 145
    sweet wines, 137
    Syrah, 31
    Trebbiano, 59
    Viognier, 56
    Zinfandel, 36, 149
Campania, 86
Canada, 111, 137
Canon-Fronsac, 65
carbonation, sparkling
    wines, 19
Carignan, 40
Casablanca Valley, 117
Cassis, 40, 77
Catalonia, 40
Cava, 91, 145
cellars, 156–9
Central Valley
    (California), 107
Chablis, 44, 45, 66–7,
    146
champagne, 15, 70–1,

144–5, 158
    bottles, 150
    glasses, 163
    grapes, 15, 23, 28, 44
    winemaking, 19
Chardonnay, 12, 43,
    44–5, 146, 150, 158
Châteauneuf-du-Pape, 23,
    31, 33, 40, 41, 58, 59,
    69, 149
Chenin Blanc, 12, 52, 147
Cheval Blanc, Château, 32
Chianti, 35, 59, 85, 148,
    150
Chile, 114–17, 118, 149
    Cabernet Sauvignon, 25
    Malbec, 39
    Merlot, 26
    Pinot Blanc, 54
    Riesling, 51
    Sémillon, 48
Chinon, 32, 73, 147
choosing wine, 144–9
Cigales, 92
Cinsault, 36, 41
Cirò, 86
Clairette de Die, 55, 145
Clare Valley, 51, 124
claret, 25, 39, 65
classifications, 153
climate, 13, 16
Clos Vougeot, 28
Colombard, 58
Condado de Huelva, 95
Condrieu, 56, 69, 147
coolers, 166
Coonawarra, 25, 124
Corbières, 40, 77
corked wine, 177
corks, 176
corkscrews, 165
Cornas, 30, 69, 149
Corton, 28
Corton-Charlemagne, 45,
    67, 146
Costers del Segre, 34, 91
Côte de Beaune, 67, 146,
    148
Côte de Blaye, 148
Côte de Bourg, 148
Côte Chalonnaise, 39, 56,

67, 146, 148
Côte de Nuits, 67, 148
Côte d'Or, 67
Côte Rôtie, 30, 56, 69,
    148
Coteaux du Layon, 52,
    147
Coteaux du Tricastin, 69
Côtes de Duras, 77
Côtes de Frontonnais, 77
Côtes de Gascogne, 146
Côtes de Provence, 77
Côtes du Rhône, 33, 69,
    148
Côtes du Rhône-Blanc, 59
Côtes du Rhône-Villages,
    40, 41, 69
Côtes du Roussillon, 40,
    77
Côtes du Ventoux, 33, 69
Crémant d'Alsace, 54, 75
Crozes-Hermitage, 30, 58,
    59, 69, 148
Curicó Valley, 117
Cuve Close, sparkling
    wines, 19

Dão, 98
decanting wine, 165, 166
dessert wines, 47, 52, 55,
    136–7, 159, 163
Dolcetto, 81
Douro, 98

Eden Valley, 51, 124
Eiswein, 103
Emilia-Romagna, 25, 26,
    37, 54, 85
England, 57, 135
Entre-Deux-Mers, 47, 65
equipment, 164–5
Erie, Lake, 110, 111
Est! Est!! Est!!!, 59
Estremadura, 99

Faugères, 77
faults, wine, 177
fermentation, 14, 19
Fino, 140, 159
Fitou, 40, 77
foil cutters, 165

food, wine and, 178–83
fortified wines, 86,
    138–41, 149, 163
France, 62–77
    Aligoté, 56
    Cabernet Franc, 32
    Cabernet Sauvignon, 25
    Chardonnay, 44–5
    Chenin Blanc, 52
    Cinsault, 41
    Colombard, 58
    Grenache, 33
    Marsanne, 59
    Merlot, 26
    Mourvèdre, 40
    Muscat, 55
    Pinot Noir, 28
    quality classifications,
        153
    Roussanne, 58
    Sauvignon Blanc, 47
    Sémillon, 48
    sparkling wines, 144–5
    Sylvaner, 55
    Syrah, 30–1
    Ugni Blanc, 59
    Viognier, 56
Franciacorta, 81
Franken, 55, 103
Franschhoek Valley, 48,
    132
Frascati, 59, 85, 146
Friuli, 26, 32, 51, 54, 82,
    83
Fronsac, 26, 65

Gaillac, 77
Gamay, 23, 39, 147
Gamay de Touraine, 39,
    147
Gard, 40, 41
Garnacha, 33, 149
Gattinara, 37, 81
Gavi, 81
Georgia, 56
Germany, 100–3
    bottles, 150
    Gewurztraminer, 53
    labels, 153
    Müller-Thurgau, 57
    Riesling, 51

Ruländer, 54
Silvaner, 55
sweet wines, 137
Weissburgunder, 54
Gevrey-Chambertin, 28,
    67, 148
Gewurztraminer, 53, 147
Ghemme, 37, 81
Gigondas, 33, 69, 149
Givry, 67, 148
glasses, 162–3
grapes, 12
    noble rot, 48, 51, 52,
        137
    red grapes, 23–41
    single varietal wines, 15
    white grapes, 43–59
Graves, 47, 48, 65
Greece, 55, 135, 137
Grenache, 33, 158
Grillet, Château, 56

Haut-Brion, Château, 65
Hawkes Bay, 39, 128
health, wine and, 176
Hérault, 40, 41
Hermitage, 30, 41, 58,
    59, 69, 147, 149
Hock, 103, 150
Hungary, 135, 137, 147
Hunter Valley, 48, 123

ice buckets, 166
Icewine, 111, 147
Internet, buying wine, 155
Israel, 40
Italy, 79–87
    Barbera, 37
    Cabernet Franc, 32
    Cabernet Sauvignon, 25
    Chardonnay, 45
    Gewurztraminer, 53
    Merlot, 26
    Müller-Thurgau, 57
    Muscat, 55
    Nebbiolo, 37
    Pinot Blanc, 54
    Pinot Grigio, 54
    quality classifications,
        153
    Riesling, 51

Sangiovese, 35
Trebbiano, 59

Jerez, 95, 140
Johannisberg Riesling, 51
Jura, 77
Jurançon, 77

Kabinett, 151

labels, 152–3
Lacryma Christi del
    Vesuvio, 86
Lambrusco, 85
Languedoc-Roussillon, 26,
    31, 33, 40, 41, 56, 58,
    76
Lazio, 85
Lebanon, 41, 135
Liebfraumilch, 57, 101,
    103, 146
Liguria, 81
Lirac, 33, 69, 149
Loire, 28, 32, 39, 47, 52,
    54, 72–3, 146, 147
Lombardy, 37, 54, 81
Lugana, 81
Luxembourg, 57

McLaren Vale, 124
Mâcon-Lugny, 67, 146
Mâconnais, 39, 56, 67,
    146
madeira, 141, 149
maderised wine, 177
Madiran, 77
mail order, buying wine,
    155
Maipo Valley, 117
Málaga, 95
Malbec, 23, 39
La Mancha, 34, 95
Manzanilla, 140, 159
Le Marche, 85
Margaret River, 125
Margaux, 65, 149
Marlborough, 28, 51, 128
Marsala, 86
Marsanne, 59, 147
Martinborough, 128
Mataro, 40

Mateus Rosé, 149
Maule Valley, 117
Médoc, 26, 32, 41, 65
Melon de Bourgogne, 54
Mendocino, 53, 107
Mendoza, 34, 35, 118
Ménétou-Salon, 47, 72
Mercurey, 67, 148
Meritage blends, 25, 32
Merlot, 12, 23, 26, 148,
    149, 150, 158
Meursault, 45, 67, 146
Mexico, 40, 54, 59
Midi, 40, 52, 59
Minervois, 40, 77
Missouri, 107
Monastrell, 40
Monbazillac, 47, 77
Mondavi, Robert, 47
Montagny, 67, 146
Montepulciano d'Abruzzo,
    85
Monterey, 53, 107
Montilla-Moriles, 95
Morey-St-Denis, 148
Moscatel de Setúbal, 55,
    99
Mosel, 103, 146, 150
Mourvèdre, 40
Müller-Thurgau, 57
Musar, Château, 41
Muscadet, 72, 146
Muscat, 55, 147, 149
Muscat de Beaumes-de-
    Venise, 55, 69, 137, 149
Muscat de Rivesaltes, 77

Napa Valley, 25, 107,
    108
Navarra, 33, 34, 91, 149
Nebbiolo, 37, 149
New South Wales, 48,
    123
New World wines, 16, 23
    (see also individual
        countries and states)
New York State, 32, 110
New Zealand, 126–9
    Cabernet Franc, 32
    Cabernet Sauvignon, 25
    Chardonnay, 45

Chenin Blanc, 52
Gewurztraminer, 53
Merlot, 26
Müller-Thurgau, 57
Pinot Noir, 28
Riesling, 51
Sauvignon Blanc, 47
sparkling wines, 145
noble rot, 48, 51, 52, 137
non-vintage (NV) wine, 16
North America, 104–11
    (see also individual
        states)
Nuits St-Georges, 28, 67,
    148

oak barrels, 14, 16, 45
oaky wines, 146–7
Oloroso, 140
Ontario, Riesling, 51
opening bottles, 166
ordering wine in
    restaurants, 169–71
Oregon, 28, 53, 54, 110
Orvieto, 59, 85, 146
Otago, Central, 128
oxidized wine, 177

Paarl, 48, 132
Pacific Northwest, 110
Palette, 40, 77
Pauillac, 65
Pedro Ximénez, 140
Pemberton, 125
Penedès, 34, 91
Penfold's Grange, 31
Pessac-Léognan, 65, 149
Petit Verdot, 23, 41
Pfalz, 53, 54, 55, 103
phylloxera, 108
Piedmont, 25, 37, 81
Pinot Blanc, 54
Pinot Grigio, 54, 146
Pinot Gris, 54, 147
Pinot Noir, 12, 15, 23,
    28, 36, 147, 148, 149,
    150, 158
Pinotage, 23, 36, 41, 149
Pomerol, 26, 65
Pommard, 28, 67, 148
port, 34, 98, 138, 141,

149, 159
Portugal, 34, 55, 96–9, 138
Pouilly-Fuissé, 45, 67, 146
Pouilly-Fumé, 47, 72, 128, 146
Priorato, 91
Prosecco, 82, 145
Provence, 40, 77, 149
Puligny-Montrachet, 45, 67, 146

Quincy, 47, 72

Rapel Valley, 117
Recioto, 82
red grapes, 12, 23–41
red wines: aging, 16
  blends, 15
  glasses, 163
  serving temperature, 167
  single varietal wines, 15
  styles, 147–9
  winemaking, 14
restaurants, ordering wine, 169–71
Retsina, 135
Reuilly, 47, 72
Rheinhessen, 55, 103
Rhine, 103, 150
Rhône Valley, 31, 33, 40, 41, 55, 56, 58, 59, 69, 148, 149
Rías Baixas, 92, 146
Ribatejo, 99
Ribera del Duero, 34, 92
Riesling, 12, 43, 51, 103, 146
Rio Negro, 118
La Rioja (Argentina), 118
Rioja (Spain), 33, 34, 40, 91, 148, 149, 150, 159
Romanée-Conti, 28
Rosé d'Anjou, 73, 149
rosé wines, 14, 33, 149
Roussanne, 58, 147
Rueda, 92
Ruländer, 54
Rully, 146, 148

Russian River Valley, 108
Rutherglen, 123, 141

St. Chinian, 77
St. Croix du Mont, 47, 65, 147
St. Emilion, 26, 32, 39, 65, 148, 149
St. Estèphe, 65, 149
St. Joseph, 30, 58, 59
St. Julien, 65
St. Péray, 58, 59
St. Véran, 67, 146
Salta, 118
San Antonio Valley, 117
San Francisco Bay, 107
San Joaquin Valley, 59
San Juan, 118
San Luis Obispo, 107
Sancerre, 28, 47, 72, 73, 128, 146
Sangiovese, 23, 35, 148
Santa Barbara County, 107
Sardinia, 86
Saumur, 32, 52, 72
Sauternes, 47, 48, 65, 137, 147
Sauvignon Blanc, 12, 43, 46–7, 48, 146, 147, 150, 158
Sauvignon de Touraine, 47
Savennières, 52
Savoie, 58, 77
screwcaps, 176
Sekt, 19, 145
Sélection de Grains Nobles, 75, 137
Sémillon, 43, 47, 48, 147, 150
serving temperature, 167
sherry, 95, 140, 149, 159
Shiraz, 149, 150
  (see also Syrah)
Sicily, 86
Sierra Foothills, 107
Silvaner, 55
single varietal wines, 15
Soave, 54, 59, 82, 146
soil, vineyards, 13
Somontano, 34, 91

Sonoma, 25, 107, 108
South Africa, 130–3
  Cabernet Franc, 32
  Cabernet Sauvignon, 25
  Chardonnay, 45
  Chenin Blanc, 52
  Cinsault, 41
  Colombard, 58
  fortified wines, 141
  Pinotage, 36, 149
  Riesling, 51
  Sémillon, 48
  Syrah, 31
South America, 112–19
  Chardonnay, 45
  Syrah, 31
  (see also individual countries)
South Australia, 124
Spain, 88–95
  Cabernet Sauvignon, 25
  Carignan, 40
  Cava, 145
  Chardonnay, 45
  Grenache, 33
  Mourvèdre, 40
  Muscat, 55
  sherry, 140
  Tempranillo, 34
sparkling wines, 144–5, 158
  bottles, 150
  Cava, 91
  champagne, 70–1
  opening bottles, 166
  winemaking, 19
Spätlese, 51, 151
Stellenbosch, 31, 132
storing wine, 160–1
styles of wine, 144–9
"Super Tuscans," 26, 35, 85
supermarkets, buying wine, 155
Swan Valley, 125
sweet wines, 51, 111, 137, 147
Switzerland, 39, 54, 55, 59, 135
Sylvaner, 55
Syrah (Shiraz), 12, 23,

30–1, 150, 158

Tartrates, 177
Tasmania, 125
tasting wine, 172–5
Tavel, 33, 69, 149
temperature, serving, 167
Tempranillo, 23, 34
terminology, tasting wine, 174
terroir, 13
Tokaji, 135, 147
Toro, 92
Touraine, 52, 54
Touriga Nacional, 149
Traminer Aromatico, 53
Trebbiano, 59
Trentino, 26, 82, 83
Trockenbeerenauslese, 51, 54, 103, 137, 147, 151
Tuscany, 25, 26, 35, 85

Uco Valley, 118
Ugni Blanc, 59
Umbria, 85
United States (see individual states)
Uruguay, 40
Utiel-Requena, 34, 95

Vacqueyras, 69
Valais, 54, 55, 59
Valdeorras, 92
Valdepeñas, 34, 95
Valencia, 40
Valle d'Aosta, 81
Valpolicella, 82, 147
vanillin, 16
vats, 14
Vega Sicilia, 33, 34, 92
Vendanges Tardives, 54, 75, 137
Veneto, 26, 54, 82
Verdicchio, 59, 85
Victoria, 59, 123, 141
Vin de Paille, 77
Vin Jaune, 77
Vin Santo, 85
vineyards, 13
Vinho Verde, 98–9
Vino Nobile di

Montepulciano, 35, 85
Vins Doux Naturels, 33, 69, 77, 137, 149
vintages, 16–17, 138, 157
Viognier, 43, 56, 147, 158
Vitis vinifera, 12
Volnay, 67, 148
Vosne-Romanée, 67
Vouvray, 52, 72, 137, 145, 146, 147

Walker Bay, 132
Washington State, 26, 32, 51, 110
Weissburgunder, 54
Wellington, 48, 132
Western Australia, 125
white grapes, 12, 43–59
white wines: aging, 16
  glasses, 163
  serving temperature, 167
  single varietal wines, 15
  styles, 146–7
  winemaking, 14
Willamette Valley, 54, 110
wine merchants, 154
winemaking, 12–19
wineries, 14
Württemberg, 54, 103

yeasts, 14
Yugoslavia, 37

Zinfandel, 23, 36, 149, 150, 158

ACKNOWLEDGMENTS

I would like to thank Alison Starling for suggesting this book in the first place, and the RPS team of Pamela Daniels, Gavin Bradshaw, Tracy Ogino, and Gabriella Le Grazie for making it happen and ensuring that it looks so beautiful. Special thanks go to my editor, Miriam "There is something of a deadline" Hyslop, for her remarkable patience, understanding, and good humor, and to Alan Williams for his stunning photographs.

Judith Murray, of Greene & Heaton, was as supportive and encouraging as always, and Chris Maybin of Berry Bros & Rudd could not have been more generous or helpful. I could not have done without the expert eyes of Susan Keevil and my old chum, David Roberts, MW: they tactfully put me right in a number of points, and any mistakes that remain are, I am ashamed to admit, all my own.

And, of course, Marina, thank you so much, yet again. I don't know how or why you put up with me.

With special thanks to Riedel Crystal.